ENDORSEMENTS

Over the years, I have had the privilege of sitting under the teaching and mentorship of Dan and longed for others to have the same experience. God answered my prayer with his book, *Leadership Alone Isn't Enough.* In these pages, you will sit elbow to elbow with him as you laugh, weep, and learn. With each devotion, you will grow in your personal leadership, be drawn closer to God's Word, and be glad you have a friend who loves you enough to share his heart.

—Tyrone Barnette, Senior Pastor, Peace Baptist Church, Decatur, Georgia

Through his forty years of leadership experience and a deep understanding of God's Word, Dan Reiland does an incredible job connecting biblical principles to the day-to-day challenges leaders face. Dan's new book, *Leadership Alone Isn't Enough,* gives practical advice to even the most experienced leaders on how a deeper relationship with God, combined with a strong leadership skill set, is critical to long-term, sustainable leadership at a high level.

—Jerry Hurley, Directional Team Leader, Team Development, Life.Church

All of us have faced the challenge of realizing we are in over our head, that who we are and what we know are simply not enough for the leadership demands that lie before us. Dan has been there and found the answers. *Leadership Alone Isn't Enough* not only speaks to the heart of my leadership, it speaks to the heart of my soul. From worry to boldness, from worship to humility, in each reading, I have been encouraged to keep going and refined into a better leader and human.

—Kadi Cole, Leadership Consultant, Executive Coach, and Author of *Developing Female Leaders* (www.kadicole.com)

One of the greatest gifts I've received in life were fourteen years under Dr. Dan Reiland's leadership. In his new book, *Leadership Alone Isn't Enough*, you're going to get the best of Dan: profound leadership insight, spiritual truths, and practical application. In the dry and weary land of leadership, God is going to use this book to renew strength in a generation of spiritual leaders and ready us for the harvest.

—Kevin Queen, Lead Pastor, Cross Point Church, Nashville, Tennessee

What an incredible gift Dan has given to leadership in the twenty-first century. I have known Dan for over thirty years, and he lives what he writes. We all know that the "monster of ministry" can devour the joy of leadership and steal our peace. In his new book, *Leadership Alone Isn't Enough*, Dan has given us a tool to walk in joy and carry the burden of leadership. I would encourage you to read slowly and thoughtfully. Answer the reflection questions. In this discipline, God will meet you and pour power and peace into your heart.

—Dr. Chris Stephens, Senior Pastor, Faith Promise Church, Knoxville, Tennessee

Dan's writings are powerful and pertinent to everyday life and leadership. In his new book, *Leadership Alone Isn't Enough*, the idea of nourishing the soul is critical to long-term effectiveness as a leader. The leadership landscape is filled with influencers who neglected their soul at great consequence. Jesus created the model for us in Luke 4:16 "as his custom (habit) was, He began to read." Communion with God for a leader isn't optional. The biblical precedent is clear: Our souls require daily encounters with God. These 40 devotions skillfully strengthen your leadership life and soul.

—Gerald Brooks DD, DCL, Pastor of Grace Church, Plano, Texas

Pastor Dan Reiland's new book, *Leadership Alone Isn't Enough*, is a powerful devotional filled with wisdom and revelation. With his typical unique insights and firsthand experiences, Dan provides a guide for the leader's journey. We know God will use this devotional to refresh and empower your life and leadership!

—Randy and Maribel Landis, Senior Pastors and Cofounders, Life Church and RINO Global Solutions, Allentown, Pennsylvania

Dan Reiland is a leader of leaders. He has a long-standing record of producing quality, practical, relevant leadership material. I have personally been blessed and encouraged by his books. And this book is no different. *Leadership Alone Isn't Enough* is a power-packed devotional designed specifically with leaders in mind. Dan does a masterful job of connecting biblical principles to leadership lessons in easy, digestible doses. I'm confident that this devotional will be a great blessing to your life, a boost to your leadership, and will prove to be time well invested!

—Virgil Sierra, Lead Pastor, Vertical Church (Iglesia Vertical), Sunrise, Florida

After almost thirty years in leadership, I have learned that leadership is much more than what you know. Real leadership comes from the unchanging truths of God's Word. Dan Reiland has once again provided tools for every leader's toolbox with these amazing devotions that will speak to your soul and reignite the leadership gift in you! Thank you, Dan, for loving and speaking to leaders!

—Mike Linch, Senior Pastor, NorthStar Church, Kennesaw, Georgia; Host of *Linch with a Leader*

Dan Reiland is an executive pastor and leadership coach with decades of experience. His new book, *Leadership Alone Isn't Enough*, is a much-needed resource for all church leaders today. Each page oozes the same authentic and personal care that you feel when you meet Dan in person. As you get drawn into the freshly crafted and God-inspired words of wisdom, it feels like you are sitting in a one-on-one mentoring session with Dan, and God is with you. Your heart and mind will be refilled, refreshed, and renewed.

—Ashley Evans, Global Senior Pastor, Influencers Church, Australia/USA/Indonesia; Author of *No More Fear*

Leadership Alone Isn't Enough, is a much-needed book for church leaders. Dan Reiland delivers the timely truth that organizational skills cannot sustain a minister of the gospel and backs it up with his shared experience and straightforward devotions that are concise, practical, and cut deep. It is a breath of fresh air that imparts biblical conviction without any of the condemnation.

—Joby Martin, Lead Pastor, The Church of Eleven 22, Jacksonville, Florida

Dan Reiland is one of those rare leadership voices that deserves your attention. Not because he commands it but because his legacy of leadership demands it. Once again, Dan profoundly and practically equips leaders in this new leadership devotional. His new book, *Leadership Alone Isn't Enough*, will encourage your heart and soul as a leader.

—Jenni Catron, Founder of The 4Sight Group, Author, Speaker

With over forty years of ministry experience, Dan Reiland knows firsthand what it means to be in the trenches of leadership. In this inspiring devotional, *Leadership Alone Isn't Enough*, Dan shares heartfelt, authentic lessons from his own journey as a leader. Each chapter will help deepen your faith, strengthen your soul, and encourage you to be more dependent on God.

—Brian Bloye, Senior Pastor, West Ridge Church, Dallas, Georgia;
Coauthor of *It's Personal—Surviving and Thriving
on the Journey of Church Planting*

I like Dan's writings because he both instructs and inspires. He instructs with everyday application supported by truth in a concise and compelling style. He also inspires the heart and the will into action. Dan's new book, *Leadership Alone Isn't Enough*, delivers again. Get a copy and sit in a quiet spot, soak in the wisdom, and invite the Holy Spirit to motivate you into action. You'll be glad you did, as these forty devotions are a great investment in your life and leadership!

—Boyd Bailey, NCF, Georgia, Wisdom Hunters, Inc.

In an era of failed leadership and unprecedented challenges, it's crucial that our families, churches, and organizations are led by leaders who are grounded in what is true. In this book, *Leadership Alone Isn't Enough*, Dan Reiland brings a fresh take on how scripture and prayer can breathe life into the soul of a leader. Personally, my heart has been refreshed!

—Tim Stevens, Executive Pastor, Willow Creek Community
Church, Chicago, Illinois; Author of *Marked by Love*

If you are a leader, you are gifted. That's a good thing. The bad thing is that over time we are all at risk of relying too much on our gifts and less on God. When that happens, it's a recipe for leadership disaster. What I love about Dan's new book, *Leadership Alone Isn't Enough*, is how he helps us recenter our leadership where it needs to be.

—Ashley Wooldridge, Senior Pastor, Christ's
Church of the Valley, Peoria, Arizona

These forty powerful devotions in Dan Reiland's new book, *Leadership Alone Isn't Enough*, reminds us as leaders that without consistent prayer, we will not hear the voice of God; and without hearing from God, we lead on our own power, which will certainly lead to burnout. Dan's writing will encourage us to have a holy boldness and go the distance for God: "After they prayed, the place where they were meeting was shaken. And they were all filled with the Holy Spirit and spoke the word of God boldly" (Acts 4:31).

—Charles Kyker, Lead Pastor, Christ Church, Hickory, North Carolina

Brad,

I appreciate you, your Kingdom-minded leadership and your friendship. And I pray these devotions are a source of great encouragement to you, your leadership and your walk with God!

Blessings,
Dan

LEADERSHIP
ALONE ISN'T ENOUGH

40 Devotions to Strengthen Your Soul

DAN REILAND

WESTBOW
PRESS®
A DIVISION OF THOMAS NELSON
& ZONDERVAN

WestBow Press books may be ordered through booksellers or by contacting:

WestBow Press
A Division of Thomas Nelson & Zondervan
1663 Liberty Drive
Bloomington, IN 47403
www.westbowpress.com
844-714-3454

Scripture quotations taken from The Holy Bible, New International Version® NIV® Copyright © 1973 1978 1984 2011 by Biblica, Inc. TM. Used by permission. All rights reserved worldwide.

ISBN: 978-1-6642-5154-0 (sc)
ISBN: 978-1-6642-5155-7 (hc)
ISBN: 978-1-6642-5153-3 (e)

Library of Congress Control Number: 2021924487

Print information available on the last page.

WestBow Press rev. date: 2/10/2022

To Patti, the love of my life.
I cherish your prayers the most.

CONTENTS

Acknowledgments xiii
Introduction: God Cannot Be Rushed xv
Best Methods: How to Benefit Most from This Devotional xix

Receive Unexpected Strength 1
Grasp Staying Power in Ministry 4
Change the Game with Gratitude 8
Wage War on Worry 12
Receive the Gift of Peace 16
Recognize Success Is God's Idea 19
Build the Foundation of Your Confidence 22
Tap into Your Power Source 26
Connect Faith and Trust 29
Take the Path of Humility 32
Measure Your Words 35
Seek God's Response to Your Problems 38
See the Real Battle 41
Embrace Bold Leadership 44
Worship Well 47
Prioritize Your First Love 51
Accept Your Divine Assignment 54
Know That God Is with You 57
Experience the Faithfulness of God 61
Prevent Burnout 65
Relish Soul-Level Rest 68
Break Free from Secrets 71
Keep Your Standards High 75
Influence through Truth 78

Lead Yourself First 81
Fight for Purity 85
Strive to Willingly Follow 89
Watch the Tone of Your Leadership 93
Embody Coachable Leadership 96
Engage Your Purpose 100
Merge Power, Love, and Leadership 103
Embrace the Gift of Wisdom 106
Find God in the Waiting 110
Build Purposeful Unity 114
Pick Up the Ministry of Reconciliation 117
Confess for the Good of Your Soul 120
Value One More Leader 123
Cultivate the Courage to Confront 126
Keep a Diligent Watch 129
Affirm Big Leadership Prayers 132

Twenty Leadership Prayers for You 137
Scripture Index 147
Other Resources by Dan Reiland 149
About the Author 153

ACKNOWLEDGMENTS

This book started out as a small and simple project. The idea was a short e-book focused on the top thirty go-to New Testament scriptures for church leaders with a little commentary for each one. As God began to guide me, the idea expanded significantly. This book of biblical devotions for leaders was challenging to write and would have never been completed without the help, patience, and expertise of others.

My heartfelt gratitude and appreciation are not easy to capture on paper, but I want to thank those who helped this book find its way to strengthen your soul.

Thank you,

Carolyn Reed Master, for the excellence you brought to this book. Your gifted writing, ideas, and brilliant ability to wordsmith a difficult phrase made a huge difference. Your grasp of scripture helped to keep my thinking on track for biblical integrity. You are a delight to work with, and I'm grateful for your passion to help develop spiritual leaders.

Bryan Mason, for your generous spirit in reviewing and commenting on the devotions from the New Testament. Your keen and experienced insights helped make it a better book. And your input on the title and subtitle was invaluable!

Jim Carpenter, for your candid comments and unique insights as you read through and reviewed the devotions from the Psalms. You definitely made them better. Your crazy big gift of creativity was a lifesaver on the title and subtitle!

Lynn Guise, for your kind willingness to lend your long-standing expertise in grammatical editing to this project. Your knowledge, experience, and precision have been truly invaluable.

WestBow Press, for your expertise, efficiency, high standards, helpful spirit in answering all my questions, and team commitment to help me produce the best and highest quality book possible.

Mackenzie Austin, for your incredibly gifted editorial eye in finding important details I never see, and your willingness to help make this a better book.

Lesley Lewis, my executive assistant, for always bringing a kind spirit, positive attitude, and can-do disposition to navigating my full schedule and helping me bring this project across the finish line.

Matthew Pless, for your consistently positive spirit, encouragement, and full-of-faith prayers. Only in heaven will we know just how much prayer made all this work!

Susan Meek, for your steadfast commitment to pray for this book to find its way to the hearts of Christian leaders.

Charlie Wetzel, for our inspiring conversations about the many facets of changing lives through the written word, and for your honest thoughts and insights about my writing.

Patti Reiland, for staying close, cheering me on, and providing great opinions on book 5. Hope you're ready for book 6!

INTRODUCTION:
GOD CANNOT BE RUSHED

Forty years of ministry have taught me that only Jesus brings real power and the life-changing authority that makes it possible for any church to reach its potential. Yet we often lead with less than that full power. It's never intentional, but it's surprisingly easy to slide into leading on your own, or at least partially on your own, especially when the pressure is on, and God doesn't seem to be moving as fast as you hope and pray.

I have prayed and pursued God for these forty years, but I have not always fully leaned into the significance of how my relationship with him impacts my leadership. Intellectually, I've known from day one that God is my source, but only decades of experience have revealed the depth of that truth. He is truly the foundation and strength of my soul, and my leadership would never reach its potential without him.

Of the thousands of church leaders I've coached over these years, so many resonate with a similar story. They love God but can become so consumed with the work of God that their walk with God isn't always what it could be. The result is that their leadership suffers. However, instead of running to God, they work harder. Sound familiar?

Please don't misunderstand. Your leadership in the local church is critical to the advancement of the Great Commission. However, leadership alone isn't enough.

A number of years ago I was leaving my prayer room in a hurry. I have come to love that little space that seems more like a private sanctuary than a simple room with a lot of books and Bibles, and yes, my guitar collection. When we built the room, I wanted to make it a place that represented both a place to pray and a place to play. I wanted it to be a place that drew even my most human side to want to be there. To make sense of that you need to know that as a young leader, I was more of a "dutiful soldier" on a mission to advance the church more than deeply knowing God. So I prayed for others and the church more than about what God wanted to do in me as his son. On some days, I'm sad to admit, prayer was closer to something on my to-do list than the incredible gift it is to connect with God in a personal and powerful way. Fortunately, I've matured some since then, but I can still get in a hurry to set out on my day to build the church.

So I was leaving my prayer room after only a short time of prayer, and I vividly remember God speaking as I walked through the doorway. He whispered, "I cannot be rushed." I stopped in my tracks, and God reassured me. "I love you; we're good. I am with you, but if you want all that I have for you, I cannot be rushed." It was true then, and it's true now. God cannot be rushed, and when I slow down to seek him, he always shows up.

It's amazing how many miracles I experience from time spent in my prayer room. I call them miracles because I've learned that nothing of eternal consequence happens from my own effort. When I wait on God, he meets me with his lovingkindness, power, favor, wisdom, and blessing. That doesn't mean he answers every prayer exactly how and when I would hope for, but he is always with me and grants me a kindness that could only come from the loving Father.

You can only lead as far as you've been led by God. In fact, to get in front of God is to risk unnecessary mistakes, a sense of misguided confidence, and the potentially dangerous outcomes of leading in your own power. And when you get behind God or out of cadence with him, you forgo the wisdom he provides to lead well through conflict, the acumen to lead with genuine confidence, and having everything you need to lead from a place of soul-level strength. We need only to walk with him.

Being led by God to lead for God brings clarity to vision, wisdom to solve problems, and supernatural favor. This divine partnership also increases faith, discernment, and conviction.

That's the purpose of this book. My goal is to help you establish a more direct connection between your relationship with God and your role as a leader. These forty devotions provide insights from biblical passages containing leadership principles. Each is written from the trenches of personal experience, candor, and from decades of coaching leaders. There are twenty-eight based on New Testament scriptures and twelve from the book of Psalms. My prayer is that they will guide you, encourage you, and strengthen you on a soul level.

BEST METHODS: HOW TO BENEFIT MOST FROM THIS DEVOTIONAL

My desire is for you to gain the most you possibly can from this collection of forty devotions. You can take any approach you like, of course, but let me briefly offer a few ideas that may enhance the value you receive from the thoughts on these pages.

1. Forty Days

   For the caffeinated leader who could not imagine taking longer than one setting per devotion, the forty-day plan, this is for you. Go for it. But let me say it's not meant to be a race. If you want to skip a day or two so you can do something different to focus your devotions, do it. Take the time you need to truly strengthen your soul. This book will be waiting for your return.

2. Forty Weeks

   For many, forty weeks will be an ideal pace. The devotions are purposefully a little longer than most and designed to be consumed more as a soak than a gulp. And similar to the forty-day plan, I encourage you to take several days each week to engage any other kind of devotional approach you like, allowing time for this content to percolate in your soul. Marinate in the reflections, and give God time to talk with you about how he wants you to respond.

3. Group Discussion

   You might really enjoy the richness and depth of conversation with a small group of three to five other leaders as you go through it on your own. My suggestion would be to meet no more than once a month, so you can discuss highlights of what you are learning from several of the devotions at a time. For example, you might cover four devotions each time you meet, answering these two questions:

   • What is God saying to you, and what are you learning?
   • How are you applying what you are learning to your leadership?

After you've gone through *Leadership Alone Isn't Enough* once, you may want to utilize the index of scriptures to refresh something that is specifically on your mind. That's the beauty of scripture; it's always fresh, alive, and new each time you read it.

The point is to choose an approach that is best for you. Again, I pray God is generous in his outpouring of grace, kindness, wisdom, and blessing upon you and your leadership.

RECEIVE UNEXPECTED STRENGTH

> But he said to me, "My grace is sufficient for you, for my power is made perfect in weakness." Therefore I will boast all the more gladly about my weaknesses, so that Christ's power may rest on me. That is why, for Christ's sake, I delight in weaknesses, in insults, in hardships, in persecutions, in difficulties. For when I am weak, then I am strong.
> —2 Corinthians 12:9–10

Can you remember a time when God asked you to step up to something big? How did it go? I can recall the moment John Maxwell asked me to be his executive pastor like it was yesterday. At that time, I served as pastor of Christian education at Skyline Church, where John was the senior pastor. The church was located in a suburb of my hometown, San Diego. I was honored and elated, but the crash soon followed.

I had not considered the reality of going from being a peer with all the staff to being their boss. That was a big oversight on my part, and though my relationships were good and my areas of ministry were doing very well, I was not a good enough leader to pull off that promotion.

Those early staff meetings were rough to say the least. I no more belonged at the head of the table than I did being an NFL quarterback. In fact, I might have been a better quarterback. Either way, I could tell I was going to get sacked.

I set the agenda and led the way, but the staff looked to John, not me. They wanted to know what he had to say, not me. What had I gotten myself into? My joy in receiving the promotion turned to panic. I didn't know what I was doing.

Even with John's encouragement and coaching, it took a long time for my confidence to grow and for the team to accept me in this role. It was well over a year before I had even the earliest sense of letting go of the training wheels. Even then I still had so much to learn. It was during that season that God began to teach me that it was in my weakness that he made me strong. I knew this principle of scripture intellectually, but it took a long time and a lot of reliance on God to see it at work in my life. I've definitely improved on this over the years, and I've continued to learn a lot. One thing I know for sure is that I'd still be weak even in my greatest moments of leadership and spiritual strength apart from God's strength at work on my behalf. How about you? Can you relate? When do you feel weak, and when do you sense God's strength? Here are two suggestions for building your strength through your walk with him:

- Choose humility rather than waiting for life to humble you. Cultivating humility is a complex idea, after all, how much humility is enough? How do you balance humility with confidence for effective leadership? These are not easy questions. We can know that no matter what level of talent, skill, and favor we have been blessed with, without God's power, all that we do comes to nothing in the course of eternity.

  That's a sobering thought, but it's also liberating because it keeps you close to God at all times. And you can know that average talent with Jesus's power resting on you is far better than superior talent on your own.

- Embrace the truth that with God you have all the strength you need.

  We know that what the apostle Paul wrote in 2 Corinthians 12:9–10 is true, but it doesn't always feel like it. Sometimes you might wonder if God is truly with you, and if he is, when will he help?

  Perhaps you've gone through some rough times financially either personally or at your church. Maybe a friend betrayed you or a large number of people left your church.

  You can feel weak and powerless, but God truly does make you strong in those times when you lean into him rather than your own ability.

  The process is one of letting go. It feels like a gigantic risk, but it's worth it. It's letting go of control and the ability to make things happen on your own. With God by your side empowering you, anything is possible. What do you need to let go of?

Reflection: When you are at your best, how do you remain dependent on God? When you are weak, what keeps you from going to God?

Notes:

GRASP STAYING POWER IN MINISTRY

> " I am the vine; you are the branches. If you remain in me and I in you, you will bear much fruit; apart from me you can do nothing. If you do not remain in me, you are like a branch that is thrown away and withers; such branches are picked up, thrown into the fire and burned. If you remain in me and my words remain in you, ask whatever you wish, and it will be done for you. This is to my Father's glory, that you bear much fruit, showing yourselves to be my disciples.
>
> —John 15:5–8

I t's often easy to start a family, but it takes effort to keep a family together. It requires intentionality to lead your family in such a way that everyone is happy, emotionally healthy, and productive.

Patti and I were married for eight years before we started our family. When our first child came along, our beautiful daughter Mackenzie, everything changed. We went from sleeping through the night, dining out, and going on date nights on a whim; to diapers, car seats, colic, all-nighters, and trips to the doctor. If you are a parent, you understand. Suddenly, thinking about what lay ahead for the next eighteen to twenty-two years seemed like a whole different journey—one that included pancakes in the VCR, imaginary friends, video games that require a PhD for Dad to play, cars driven into mailboxes, and college tuition that rivaled the national debt. But of course, being a parent also comes with lots of joy.

In the same way, it's easy to start out in ministry with one picture in mind, but then an entirely different story emerges, requiring increased staying power. As with your kids, seeing people change and grow does bring a lot of wonderful joy and is so richly rewarding. But ministry, like family, is not without challenges, risks, setbacks, and complications. God's Word is clear that when we fail to remain connected to the vine, Jesus, we can accomplish nothing. In order to stay connected, we must seek the heart and wisdom of God through the power and presence of Jesus.

In connection to the vine, I believe there are two other things that, when combined, give you great staying power. They are fruit and joy.

FRUIT

Jesus spoke clearly about bearing or producing much fruit in John 15. The reference is to results or productivity, and the idea is one of measurable eternal outcomes. Kingdom results are spiritual in nature, and you can't force them. However, that does not make them fuzzy or unclear. In the same way, spiritual outcomes are not subjective merely because they involve people. The following examples represent the fruit of your leadership:

- One person saying yes to Jesus is measurable.
- Recruiting one small group leader is quantifiable.
- A rocky marriage restored to health is clear for all to see.

JOY

Ministry may be easy when it begins, but over the long haul, it never remains that way. In fact, you may experience days and even extended seasons of difficult challenges and stress in ministry or at home. But even in those tough times, you can still experience a deep and abiding joy. Joy is listed as a fruit of the spirit in Galatians 5:22–23. This means it's a promise to you that is part of the Spirit within you. Don't let ministry steal it from you.

You must have both fruit and joy. If you have one without the other for any length of time, your leadership experience begins to suffer.

- Fruit without joy is drudgery.
  Results without joy are too heavy a burden for anyone to carry because without joy, you cannot last in ministry. Every leader needs to cultivate a sense of inner joy. Joy is cultivated by loving the people you work with, loving your job, and loving God. Gratitude and a positive attitude also play a big part.

- Joy without fruit is barren.
  Joy without results is a fun party, but in terms of your leadership efforts, it is essentially a waste of time because it's a shallow endeavor. God designed us to be productive as leaders, and productivity (fruit) is enhanced by growing as a leader in combination with focused, consistent hard work and abiding in Jesus.

You simply cannot go the distance without both fruit and joy.

Reflection: How would you describe the level of fruit and joy in your ministry life? Which is greater for you right now, fruit or joy, and how can you bring them back into balance?

Notes:

CHANGE THE GAME
WITH GRATITUDE

> Shout for joy to the LORD, all the earth. Worship the LORD with gladness; come before him with joyful songs. Know that the LORD is God. It is he who made us, and we are his; we are his people, the sheep of his pasture. Enter his gates with thanksgiving and his courts with praise; give thanks to him and praise his name. For the LORD is good and his love endures forever; his faithfulness continues through all generations.
>
> —Psalm 100

Worship and gratitude are closely connected. We worship God because he is God. Additionally, we are grateful for all his blessings, so we come before him with our thanksgiving!

Gratitude and thanksgiving are also closely intertwined. Gratitude represents the disposition of your heart, and communicating thanks is an outward expression of your gratitude.

The devil loves it when we lack gratitude. When we are unhappy with what we have and merely want more, we are positioned perfectly for one of his biggest attacks on us as Christian leaders—discouragement.

"An ungrateful soul is an empty soul because it always wants more."[1] The drive for more often plagues us as leaders. Wanting more, however, isn't always a detriment to your soul. More salvations, more baptisms, more people set free from addiction are good things to desire. However, there is a subtle but powerful desire that can move your heart just enough to rob you of your gratitude even when you see and sense God at work because it's still not enough for you. This is where discouragement seeps in and trips you up.

It's a tricky place for you as a leader. The drive for growth is part of what makes you a good leader. However, it becomes a problem when it turns into an insatiable desire that drives you to treat people differently and ultimately causes you to lose your inner peace and joy.

In chapter 5 of my book *Confident Leader!* I talk about the difference between being content and being satisfied. Here's a brief excerpt: "Lack of inner contentment comes when God and I are out of sync. The problem is not my drive for new territory; it is when I think things should be bigger and move faster than God does."[2]

Gratitude isn't a skill to be improved. It's a disposition or quality of your soul to be cultivated. It finds its outward expression by giving thanks primarily in two large areas: first, to God for who he is; and second, to God for all that you have.

- Gratitude to God
  The magnitude of God deserves our constant gratitude. Consider just a few of the many gifts he gives us, including his love, faithfulness, mercy, kindness, truth, justice, and provision. Then as we expand our thoughts about God, for example, to include the fullness of the Trinity, our gratitude increases. The Father, Son, and Holy Spirit are one, yet they are distinct.

---

[1] Dan Reiland, *Confident Leader!: Become One, Stay One* (Nashville: Thomas Nelson, 2020), 61.
[2] Ibid.

When I consider the distinctives of the Trinity, I find that my thanksgiving becomes more specific. For example, I often thank God for his unfailing love and the beauty of creation. I thank Jesus for my salvation and every good and perfect gift. And I thank the Holy Spirit for wisdom, comfort, and spiritual authority. Yes, you can simply say Lord or Father in Heaven for all these things and more, but you might find this practice helpful to maintain a freshness in your expression of gratitude.

While thanking God for the difficult experiences in life can be challenging, expressing gratitude for the strength to get through them and the resulting personal growth we experience is equally important.

• Gratitude for all that you have
  It's easy to slip from a place of gratitude into discontentment. When your eyes see and focus on what you don't have, it's a fast slope downward from there. I've tripped down that slope more times than I care to admit.

A common slide for me is comparing. When I walk into a friend's home that is big, beautiful, and nearly makes me gasp from how impressive it is, I am genuinely happy for them, but I may still compare it to where I live. That's a mistake. There will always be lots of bigger and better homes. Here's my reality: Patti and I live in a wonderful house; it's the comparison that gets me in trouble and can cause me to lose perspective. How about you? What trips you up?

Reflection: What are three things you are truly grateful for that normally don't come to mind?

Notes:

WAGE WAR ON WORRY

> But seek first his kingdom and his righteousness, and all these things will be given to you as well. Therefore do not worry about tomorrow, for tomorrow will worry about itself. Each day has enough trouble of its own.
> —Matthew 6:33–34

Worry is a waste of time, and we know it. Yet, we still worry about stuff. We worry about our kids, problems at work, money matters, health issues, and who will be elected to office. We worry about big things and little things, but mostly we worry about things that never happen.

Being follically challenged and growing up in Southern California means I received more than my share of sunshine. I've had skin cancer on the top of my head twice now. Both times the doctor used a surgical technique called Mohs and declared me all clear. Nonetheless, the first time I had skin cancer, I worried about what might happen if it came back. The second time, I worried about getting it a third time. Do you see the pattern? Worrying about this is nothing more than wasted thoughts. A better remedy is to use sunblock, wear a hat, and get on with life!

The real problem with worry is that it consumes productive

energy and leaves you with little to show for your time except an inability to focus, a lack of confidence, and emotional exhaustion. "What if?" is the battle cry of a leader who worries. "What if the income doesn't come back up?" "What if we don't get the certificate of occupancy by grand opening?" "What if my leadership isn't accepted?" While some contingency planning is good for strategy, it's not a remedy for worry.

Consider Jesus's words in Luke 12:25: "Who of you by worrying can add a single hour to your life?" The answer is none of us! Worry never adds value to your situation. Nor does it do anything to strengthen your soul.

In fact, if we don't wage war on worry, the enemy actually has room to advance in stealthy ways to take soul territory.

- Worry erodes your trust in God.
  It's difficult to develop faith when you worry because they are contradictory concepts. Worry is focused on something undesirable that *might* happen, while faith is focused on the potential for a positive outcome based on God's provision. God isn't obligated to "perform" for us, but he has proven worthy of our trust and faith. In fact, there's never been a time when God made a mistake.

- Worry dilutes your ability to serve and give yourself to others. Worry, like an illness, shrinks your world. The greater the illness, the smaller your world. When you're really sick, your focus is solely on yourself. It's not that you're selfish; you're simply consumed! Your heart and mind may still desire to give of yourself to others, but significant worry can considerably diminish your capacity to give.

- Worry zaps you of physical, emotional, and mental energy. Worry is like leaving your flashlight permanently on. The battery that was designed to last for a long time with normal usage is completely drained in a couple of days. The light slowly grows dim and then flickers out. Likewise, worry drains your personal battery in a very short time. When operating your human engine in healthy ways, your God-given energy will cover all your needs.

Waging war on worry requires action. First, confess that what you're worried about hasn't happened, and acknowledge that every minute thinking about it is lost. Second, take action on what you can change. What you can't change isn't a problem. It's a fact of life that calls for you to adapt, not alter reality.

The enemy would love to steal your heart's focus and take up residence in your soul. Guard your heart, and trade lies for truth. When you are plagued by worrisome thoughts, try to replace them with the following truths:

- God hasn't forgotten you; he's always with you.
  Through the promise of scripture and life experience, you know God is with you even if it doesn't always feel like it. Meditate on that truth.

- You haven't been given more than you can handle.
  God promises to give you strength, and when your problems seem overwhelming, the Holy Spirit comforts you.

- You're not alone; there are always people who care about you.
  God's presence takes on human form through friends and family. Don't overlook this significant blessing. Lean into their love and care.

Reflection: What are you worried about today for which you can trust God?

Notes:

RECEIVE THE GIFT OF PEACE

> But the Advocate, the Holy Spirit, whom the Father will send in my name, will teach you all things and will remind you of everything I have said to you. Peace I leave with you; my peace I give you. I do not give to you as the world gives. Do not let your hearts be troubled and do not be afraid.
>
> —John 14:26–27

As I write this devotion, I'm sitting in the waiting room while my wife, Patti, is in surgery. It's a routine surgery but for an unusual circumstance. One of her tonsils grew back. The ENT recommended it be removed because in an unlikely case, it could become something more serious. As you can imagine, my peace is being challenged today.

As a spiritual leader, I want to say, "God's got this. I'm at complete peace." And I do know God is with us, but I can't say I'm at complete peace in the moment. The good news is that God and I have a few hours to work on this together.

These things never really get easier, do they? No matter how many trials we must face as leaders, we are human, and life can throw us curve balls that catch us off guard. I don't believe these surprises are representative of some lack in me as a leader, but they do remind me that leadership alone is never enough to strengthen my soul. I need God to fill the gaps and shore up the limitations of my perspectives with his peace.

How about you? Is there anything that's challenging your peace today? It might be a financial problem, a health concern, something with a family relationship, or your ministry. Just recently I spoke to a young couple whose two-year-old daughter had a seizure. There's no history of seizures or anything else that points to why this happened. Now the tests begin, and their peace is being challenged.

In addition to difficult personal issues, ministry also can rob you of your peace. Things don't always go as planned. People get upset. Attendance drops. The roof leaks, and there's no room in the budget to repair it. You trust that God is with you, but to always have peace, not so much.

Being reminded to "not let your hearts be troubled" (John 14:1) always seems like a beautiful combination of a comforting feeling and easier said than done. While it's hard to manage your heart's temperament, it's comforting to remember that Jesus said that to personally bring us a message of peace. I try to imagine him sitting with me and quietly saying those words. Do you?

In addition to Jesus's message of peace to you, the promise of the Holy Spirit brings personal power to what he said. The Advocate, whom Jesus sent, is with you. He is present, powerful, and comforting. You can lean into him.

The next phrase in our Scripture brings it home. The Holy Spirit reminds us of everything Jesus said and teaches us all we need to know. That brings peace because we don't need to seek anything beyond what Jesus gives us.

Jesus then says, "Peace I leave with you; my peace I give you." That's a promise we can hold onto when we find ourselves grasping for peace. Jesus also says in John 16:33, "I have told you these things, so that in me you may have peace. In this world you will have trouble. But take heart! I have overcome the world."

Two practical thoughts about peace:

- We don't need to know the future to have peace in the present.

  I'd like to know the results of Patti's surgery, but I need to wait. Life was designed to be lived in the present. Peace is found in the now, not in wondering about the future. It's difficult to remain in the present, but that's where we experience the deepest meaning, the most genuine joy, and the fullness of the presence of God.

- We don't need to carry what we can't control.

  Peace is lost when we focus on what we can't control. Peace is at risk when we attempt to carry more than God wants us to carry. Peace is found when we sit in the love of God and trust him at his word. "Now may the Lord of peace himself give you peace at all times and in every way" (2 Thessalonians 3:16).

Reflection: What can you let go of in the future and grab hold of in the present to strengthen your peace?

Notes:

RECOGNIZE SUCCESS IS GOD'S IDEA

> Now this I know: The LORD gives victory to his anointed. He answers him from his heavenly sanctuary with the victorious power of his right hand. Some trust in chariots and some in horses, but we trust in the name of the LORD our God. They are brought to their knees and fall, but we rise up and stand firm. LORD, give victory to the king! Answer us when we call!
> —Psalm 20:6–9

We all prefer victory over defeat. However, seeking God's power for ministry success begins with the willingness to accept whatever comes. When we sign up to serve, we're in ministry to glorify God, and our personal blessings are extra. Candidly, that's not always easy to accept, and it's essentially the meaning of, "pick up your cross."

I'm not suggesting that God is the author of failure in your life. But at times, life and leadership are difficult, and he may choose to use that for your good. Even more complex, God may define success, or failure, differently than you do.

Are you willing to risk failure to achieve success? I know that's a big question, but you must risk setbacks to realize forward motion and momentum. When any NFL team takes the field, the players know they could lose. They know they will take hits and even face injuries, but that's the price of the success they desire—to win the game. What price are you willing to pay?

Success is a godly idea (Joshua 1:7), but what is involved in attaining it?

- Success is never found on the sidelines.
  If you've been in leadership for a while, the accumulation of hits can make you head for the sidelines, maybe not literally but at a heart and passion level. You might be tempted to pull back that last 10 percent in your teaching, the last bit that really needs to be said, but that's often where the Holy Spirit shows up. You might consider riding the make-no-waves position in your decision-making, but that won't help you make progress.

  Victory is only found amid the battle. Success requires being fully engaged in the game. Are you all in? Is there any place you might be playing it safe or holding back?

- Know what you won't sacrifice.
  We've already considered the need for sacrifice, but it's important to consider the other side. What will you *not* sacrifice for the sake of so-called success? You can probably name at least one or two of your friends or acquaintances who have lost their way in their pursuit of success.

  It's a slippery slope that can get a foothold in a number of ways. Dealing with significant and sustained pressure can result in a decline in your standards. Typically, however, it begins to reveal itself in an erosion of your values. It's a very subtle descent. No leader wakes up one day deciding to abandon his or her family or engage in lying, cheating, or stealing. It starts by bending your values to either get what you want or relieve the pressure you are feeling. We all need to take an inventory of the values we hold dear and then guard them and stay true to them.

- Allow God to define success.
  For the longest time I wrestled with the idea of who determines the level or definition of my success. I'm not talking about success in a theological or intellectual way; I know God is in control, and I definitely want his will over mine. The wrestling I'm referring to is in how it works out from day to day. When it comes to the strength, growth, and impact of the church, it's not always clear what God has in mind.

  Accordingly, the God-given drive within me creates tension. The drive for more spiritual territory through realizing the vision and seeing more changed lives makes me want to take success in my own hands. And I must often rest in the fact that the church may be exactly where God wants it to be in any given moment.

  The challenge for you and me is to let God define success and trust that he is at work. Ultimately, success is about trust. Determine where you place your trust. "Some trust in chariots and some in horses, but we trust in the name of the LORD our God" (Psalm 20:7).

Reflection: Do you have a sense that you and God are aligned and on track with the definition of success in your life? How are you assured of this?

Notes:

BUILD THE FOUNDATION OF YOUR CONFIDENCE

> Such confidence we have through Christ before God. Not that we are competent in ourselves to claim anything for ourselves, but our competence comes from God. He has made us competent as ministers of a new covenant—not of the letter but of the Spirit; for the letter kills, but the Spirit gives life.
>
> —2 Corinthians 3:4–6

Confidence is desired by all leaders, but many experience it inconsistently. There is a big difference between writing a talk in your study and stepping up to deliver it. Suddenly your brilliant outline faces the reality of a crowd of people who will have their own opinions. Or the vision that you were certain of a day before is put to the test when you walk into the boardroom.

So how can you unpack that experience through the lens of 2 Corinthians 3:4–6? What is the difference between confidence and competence? How are they connected?

Confidence and competence are closely intertwined and dependent on each other for results. Additionally, the knowledge that our competence comes from God and our confidence is through Christ keeps the two concepts tightly connected.

I'm sure that you've experienced what it's like to lack competence and, therefore, lose your confidence. For example, you may have faced a big problem and just didn't know what to do to move forward. Remember, not knowing what to do doesn't mean you don't know what you're doing.

In parallel, you've likely also experienced a time when you lacked leadership confidence so much that you didn't deliver on skills and abilities you knew you had. For example, you may have been communicating a new vision that stretched your own faith, and because of that, your natural communication skills were thrown off track. Remember, not being your best in the moment doesn't mean you won't be again in the future.

Ultimately, your confidence as a leader is found in Christ, but there is a part you own as well. From conquering fears and insecurities to believing in yourself and developing your God-given talents, you partner with God in your confidence. That may seem challenging, but the good news is that God is the ultimate source of your confidence. So when it's lacking, you can rely on him to do what you cannot do.

A quick, big-picture look at how you and God partner together in the development of consistent and authentic confidence includes these three categories:

- Identity in Christ
  There is a unique genetic code that belongs only to you. It's part of creation. The color of your eyes, your personality, and even some of your mannerisms are hardwired into who you are. But as a Christ-follower, the core of your identity is that you are a new creation who is loved and valued by God. Your sins are forgiven, and you are invited to live in the grace of God. All of that establishes the foundation of who you are.

  Living in this truth is a grand invitation and an incredible opportunity. It's easy to take all this for granted, but to miss it would be like finding out you actually have different birth parents. Your identity would be shaken, to say the least, because you simply wouldn't know who you really are, which would inevitably have an impact on your confidence. Your identity shapes your thought process, decision-making, and your choices.

- Gifts and calling
  You have been created on purpose with a purpose. This is one of God's great gifts to you. Further, you have been given specific spiritual gifts and unique human talents and abilities. Take the opportunity to express gratitude to God right now as you think and pray. Don't let the enemy whisper lies to you that deny your gifts and abilities or steal your confidence!

  What you do with all God has given you is a matter of stewardship, and it's connected to your calling as a Christian leader. You've been called to serve in ministry, so remember and reflect on when God made that clear to you. Sometimes that reminder is the best confidence boost you can receive.

- Practice and experience
  Competence does matter. If it didn't matter, God would not have given you gifts, opportunities, and the ability to improve. Your development as a leader is a lifetime process, but I encourage you to quietly reflect on what you are doing now to honor God's design and purpose for you. What are you working on specifically to improve as a leader in order to reach the potential he has placed in you? The better you become, the stronger your confidence will grow. My book *Confident Leader!* may be a good resource for you.

Reflection: In one word, how would you describe your confidence? Which of the above three points needs your attention most?

Notes:

TAP INTO YOUR POWER SOURCE

> "But you will receive power when the Holy Spirit comes on you; and you will be witnesses in Jerusalem, and in all Judea and Samaria, and to the ends of the earth."
>
> —Acts 1:8

A t times, most of us feel as if our ministries are a little bigger than we can handle. This is as it should be. It doesn't reflect incompetence but instead, dependence. If we had all the answers, there would be no risk, and if the outcomes were certain, there would be no real leadership taking place.

The Lewis and Clark expedition in the early 1800s was the first American expedition to cross the western portion of the United States. The Corps of Discovery was a select group of hearty, eager explorers under the co-command of Meriwether Lewis and his friend, William Clark.[3] They explored truly "off the map," figuring it out as they went. Just like their journey, we, too, are constantly going where we've never gone before. After all, that's the essence of leadership.

Kevin Myers, the senior pastor of 12Stone Church, and I have

---

[3] Hadley Mears, "Lewis and Clark: How the Corps of Discovery Transformed North America," Biography.com, accessed November 21, 2021, https://www. biography.com/news/lewis-clark-corps-of-discovery-sacagawea.

often smiled and described our twenty years together as something like a Lewis and Clark expedition. We are exploring off the map to places in ministry we've never been before. One thing we know for sure: There is no going back!

You're a trailblazer too! Others may be ahead of you on your leadership journey, just like others are ahead of us, but what remains true is that your journey is new to you.

In the same way that Lewis and Clark were gifted leaders, each with his own unique set of skills backed by passion and commitment, there is a great deal of ministry that can be done with your human talent. Yes, there is a power that comes from being good at what you do, but in ministry, that's not enough. You have probably realized that without God's presence and power, your ministry is not going to work—at least certainly not on an eternal level.

Despite all that, we often try to set out on our own anyway. I have. What about you? Sometimes it's easy to grow weary waiting on God to do what only he can do, so we run ahead of his timing. Other times we think we have enough strength in our reserves to push an agenda. The truth is we could have done so much more if we had waited for God to enhance our abilities and giftedness. Are you tempted to rush into what you know how to do? Are you perhaps lacking the power that comes from time with God, surrender, and obedience?

The promise of Acts 1:8 is that the Holy Spirit brings power, but don't miss that the power is directly connected to carrying the good news of Christ to all who do not know him. Evangelism is at the core of all ministry. However, this promised power is not limited specifically to evangelism. The thought here carries a larger scope encompassing the fullness of your ministry, including personal "power" for your leadership and your discipleship efforts as long as they remain in alignment with God's plan. This is commonly referred to as God's favor.

The point is to remember the source of your power. It's not you. There is so much freedom and liberation in that truth. You don't have to make happen what you can't make happen! That's not a theological recipe for excuses; it's the reality of your dependence on God. It allows you to breathe a sigh of relief and fills your soul with hope that your efforts really can make a difference.

There is no secret formula for God's power. It has already been freely given. However, there are pathways that increase your availability and ability to receive that power:

- Surrender to his will
  Make it about God's agenda, not yours. That's not always as easy as it sounds. It begins with hearing his voice to know his plan rather than making your plan first.

- Obedience to his prompts
  Sometimes God's prompts don't make sense. For example, I've been under financial pressure, and yet God asked me to give more. That is highly likely connected to making myself available to his power over mine.

- Dependence on his favor
  Honest soul-searching to know whose power you are operating on is always appropriate.

Reflection: In what areas do you find yourself depending on your own strength? What do you need to do to rely on God instead?

Notes:

CONNECT FAITH AND TRUST

> Trust in the Lord, and do good; dwell in the land and enjoy safe pasture. Take delight in the Lord, and he will give you the desires of your heart. Commit your way to the Lord; trust in him and he will do this: He will make your righteous reward shine like the dawn, your vindication like the noonday sun. Be still before the Lord and wait patiently for him; do not fret when people succeed in their ways, when they carry out their wicked schemes.
>
> —Psalm 37:3–7

Faith and trust are closely connected. In fact, they are difficult to separate. If you will allow me some leeway, I'd like to give it a try to give us more clarity within the context of this devotion.

- Faith dwells more in the spiritual realm.
  "For we live by faith, not by sight" (2 Corinthians 5:7).
  Living by faith means to live your life in light of eternal outcomes. That's an entirely different measurement than strictly living within the natural realm. Living by faith requires specific risks and decisions that shape how you live according to God's will. There are no promises in life, but we have faith that God is with us now and will be for eternity. That is a prospect of faith.

As I write these words, a dear friend of mine, Janene, is undergoing treatment for cancer. She is believing God for her healing and has faith in his love and her eternal destiny. She doesn't get to make the decision for her healing, but she has faith in God. When the stakes are high, as they are for Janene, your faith can be greatly tested. How has your faith been tested in last six months or so?

- Trust lives more in the natural realm.
  We've already acknowledged that faith and trust are closely intertwined, but let me take a slightly different slant with the concept of trust. While your worldview is based on what is eternal, you live your physical life in the here and now. You eat, sleep, and need shelter. You need money to cover your basic necessities and even some of the wonderful enjoyment that life offers you. You trust that God provides these things.

When your trust in God breaks down, it's easy to want to take control back from him. It's not usually a willful or instantaneous switch. It's often gradual and very subtle. But it is easy to do. I've seen this when pastoral leaders experience financial pressure, and the tone of their preaching changes. You can sense their desperation and feel their pressure as it leaks out through their words and disposition. Rather than inviting their congregation to be generous, they begin to push them to give. In contrast, when you trust God, you prepare to your best ability, pray like crazy, teach biblical truth boldly, and then trust God with the results.

Faith always leads me back to trust. If I focus on eternity, my faith muscles build my trust. If I become myopically focused on the here and now, my faith fades, and I stumble over trust. Inevitably, I then take leadership into my own hands. How foolish. I know that doesn't work, but the temptation remains. How has your level of trust been these past few months?

After addressing faith and trust, the psalmist speaks to stillness: "Be still before the Lord" (Psalm 37:7). This has two applications, and both are important.

- A physical stillness
  I love my little prayer room in the basement of our home. My small, old wooden desk covered with books and Bibles faces a window looking out into the gardens. It's a place where I can be separated from life's distractions and be physically still before God. I don't mean completely motionless. I often get up from my chair to walk in small circles as I pray. But it's a physical stillness compared to a fast-paced schedule of leadership demands for the day.

- A stillness within your soul
  The leadership challenges of each day often cause stress or anxiety, which can cause your stillness before God to evaporate quickly. Faith and trust can be like a vapor. When you possess a stillness within your soul because of the consistency of your faith and trust, your soul is at peace. Fret is gone, and faith is present.

Being still takes the worry and anxiousness out of faith and trust. As a result, delight in God increases.

Reflection: What is the most significant thing that potentially dulls your faith or lessens your trust today? What is your first step to breakthrough?

Notes:

TAKE THE PATH OF HUMILITY

> Jesus called them together and said, "You know that those who are regarded as rulers of the Gentiles lord it over them, and their high officials exercise authority over them. Not so with you. Instead, whoever wants to become great among you must be your servant, and whoever wants to be first must be slave of all. For even the Son of Man did not come to be served, but to serve, and to give his life as a ransom for many."
>
> —Mark 10:42–45

Jesus modeled these verses for us by taking the form of a man, humbling himself, and assuming the nature of a servant. He possessed the nature of God but did not demand that authority or power (Philippians 2:6). Instead, he gave himself for us.

The path of humility isn't an easy road. It involves a constant emptying of self and assuming of the role of a servant. It's not merely a humble attitude. After all, Jesus washed the disciples' feet (John 13:1–17). Humility without serving others becomes hollow and empty over time. In extreme cases, Jesus called it hypocrisy. This is not a thought that hints at works, or worse, legalism, but at a heart that eagerly embraces humility over hubris.

Personally, I prefer the path of humility over the discipline of being humbled. Life guarantees that the proud will be humbled, and that's a more difficult road to travel. Of course the moment we assume we have a measure of success in gaining humility, we're already in trouble again.

In my current role as chief of staff, I regularly travel on Sundays to our campuses to coach and encourage our teams. It takes weeks to see all seven of our campuses. Whether it's interacting with team members I don't get to see often, receiving warm, "We love it when you're here," greetings, or bantering with the volunteer team in the parking lot, I always love my campus visits.

During a visit to one of the campuses I hadn't been to in some time, I was welcomed by one of our greeters, handed a bulletin, and asked how long I had been attending 12Stone. That caught me off guard because after all, I had been on the team for nineteen years. I started to point toward my name badge, which included my title, to introduce myself, but I hadn't put it on that day.

Needless to say, it didn't take long for me to realize that my back-of-the-room position of leadership had limited my exposure to our growing congregation. In that moment, I felt an odd sense of obscurity. Thankfully, however, that humorous exchange provided a little needed humility. I smiled and thanked her for the bulletin.

We can avoid pride by pursuing humility. Ultimately, humility means you don't feel superior to others, and you don't have a need to behave as if you are superior to others. And when we don't pursue humility, our hearts get revealed in two ways:

- Our hearts get revealed quickly in situations when the stakes are high, such as not getting invited to an important meeting or not receiving a promotion we had expected. What begins to bubble and burn inside reveals much of the pride we harbor.
- Our hearts are also revealed in the daily confrontation with little things. For example, when someone cuts into the line in front of me, what goes on inside me? *They should be behind me! I was here first!* In terms of social decorum, there

may be some truth to that thought, but in terms of humility, the pride in my heart just got revealed.

Whether the issue is big or small, pride is a prison. Humility leads to freedom. Pride grabs for more and holds on. Humility holds life loosely and gives much. Pride assumes entitlement. Humility expresses gratitude. Pride weighs you down. Humility opens the door to being lifted up according to God's plan (1 Peter 5:6).

There's great strength in humility because it's founded in God's truth and backed by his promises. Humility strengthens our souls by making us more like Christ, providing greater personal security and bringing freedom to lead from a position of love and natural influence rather than authority.

Becoming more humble is a work of awareness coupled with intention. But it's important to remember that humility isn't something to achieve; it's a lifestyle to embrace. The more genuine your humility, the less aware of it you are, and the more your leadership takes on the quality of a servant. Naturally, our humanity may prevent humility at times, but as we change our thoughts about serving, become more cognizant of the opportunities to care for others from our positions of leadership, and begin to experience joy in doing so, we will get on the right path to leading with humility.

Reflection: What are the identifying characteristics of humility in your leadership?

Notes:

MEASURE YOUR WORDS

> Do not let any unwholesome talk come out of your mouths, but only what is helpful for building others up according to their needs, that it may benefit those who listen.
>
> —Ephesians 4:29

Words either build others up or tear them down. Therefore, they have the power to either enhance a leader's influence or prohibit him or her from leading others well.

Further, we all know good leadership in the church or in business starts with good leadership in one's home. Words spoken in our most unguarded moments are very revealing. We all make mistakes and fall short at times, but we can do better. Sharp words to our kids or critical words to our spouses always end up hurting those we love most. The goal is that those word choices not become patterns that leave us with regret.

A young leader in his thirties opened up about being critical toward his wife and two kids. He loves his family, provides well, and would never intentionally hurt them. Yet, the pressure of his work was getting to him, and it came out at home, when he was most tired. He's a verbal guy, and all too often the criticism found its way out in words, and for extended periods of time. It came to a head one evening after a particularly difficult day at work. When he arrived home, the house was a mess, the kids were upset and arguing with each other, and his wife forgot to take one of the kids to the dentist after school. His words to her were, "What is it that you do all day?" That was it. She was deeply hurt, and an argument ensued. When tempers calmed, she explained to him how words like that completely devalued her as a person and demotivated her to keep up with the chaotic schedule of a busy stay-at-home mom. They worked through it, but it took time as his words had worn her down.

Words matter. James 3:9 reminds us that "With the tongue we praise our Lord and Father, and with it we curse human beings, who have been made in God's likeness." The duplicity of the tongue can get us in trouble if we are not careful.

It's not only in our homes and for those we lead, but our words are also important as we talk with those who do not follow Christ. Consider the words of the apostle Paul, "Let your conversation be always full of grace, seasoned with salt, so that you may know how to answer everyone" (Colossians 4:6). This is especially true of those who are skeptical of Christianity because of the hypocrisy they see in the faith community.

Even King David was aware of his own struggle with the words he used when he wrote, "Set a guard over my mouth, LORD; keep watch over the door of my lips. Do not let my heart be drawn to what is evil so that I take part in wicked deeds along with those who are evildoers; do not let me eat their delicacies" (Psalm 141:3–4). We are all inclined to speak evil if we are not vigilant about what we allow to take root in our hearts.

In contrast to the young business leader's story, imagine the uplifted spirit of a spouse who receives a regular diet of empowering words. Or picture the glow on a child's face when receiving encouraging words. Think about the maturing of character in a teenager who lived up to the words of affirmation received from a parent. Consistency and a wise choice of words are difficult but worth our effort in order to make our relationships healthy.

Practical Steps toward Using Words of Affirmation:

- Consider what is going on in your heart.
  Are your words just the result of a bad day or crazy high pressure? Or is the Holy Spirit trying to alert you about something deeper? From getting some rest to the forgiveness of sin, the range of remedy is large.

- Think before you speak.
  Choose your words wisely. That's not always easy in the middle of an intense conversation, but there are some simple things that are helpful. One thing that works well is silently counting to three before you speak. Another is to decide before the conversation that you want to add value and to encourage rather than tear down.

- If you have offended or hurt someone with your words, make it right.
  Does anyone come to mind whom you need to apologize to this week?

Reflection: In what ways may God want to refine the condition of your heart, so your words are as consistently uplifting as possible?

Notes:

SEEK GOD'S RESPONSE TO YOUR PROBLEMS

> I sought the LORD, and he answered me; he delivered me from all my fears. Those who look to him are radiant; their faces are never covered with shame. This poor man called, and the LORD heard him; he saved him out of all his troubles. The angel of the LORD encamps around those who fear him, and he delivers them. Taste and see that the LORD is good; blessed is the one who takes refuge in him.
>
> —Psalm 34:4–8

As a leader, you are expected to be strong-minded, strategic, courageous, and deliberate in decision-making. You are also expected to care for the people you lead with the compassion of a good shepherd and comfort those who are hurting.

What do you do, however, when *you* are the one hurting? Where do you go and to whom do you talk? Having good friends always makes a big difference, but there are moments, more often than you might care to admit, when only God can carry you through to the other side of your troubles. "The righteous cry out, and the LORD hears them; he delivers them from all their troubles. The LORD is close to the brokenhearted and saves those who are crushed in spirit. The righteous person may have many troubles, but the LORD delivers him from them all" (Psalm 34:17–19).

I know a wonderful volunteer in his home church who lost his daughter to a substance addiction. He was crushed. It's been years now, and he still tears up when he talks about it. He misses his daughter every day. He even describes it as having a hole in his heart and says that if he lets himself dwell on the emptiness, it's hard to catch his breath. Fortunately, he has a great family, friends, and support system. He does well most of the time, but there are moments when the pain surfaces. It overwhelms him and crushes his spirit. It is in those moments that God reminds him of his purpose, gives him the power to keep going, and comforts him with the Holy Spirit. All of this brings him great peace.

Not every heartbreaking moment we experience is that traumatic, but it's unlikely that you will escape the need for God's comfort at some point. In my years of ministry, I've experienced hurt in the form of betrayal that helped me understand what my friend meant when he said, "It's hard to catch my breath." Retaliation or revenge is wrong. Pretending it's no big deal is not healthy. Allowing anger or bitterness to fester is a big mistake. Talking with close mentors was invaluable. But in the end, God walked me through it.

How about you? What hurts have you experienced that made it "hard to breathe?" How did you handle them? Are you healed, whole, and healthy?

What is your practice in taking the weighty things of life to God? Here's a helpful pathway for you to consider.

- Don't delay.
  One of the biggest missteps you can take is to delay dealing with the hurt. From shear pain to the pressures of current demands, you may feel incapable of even thinking about it. It's not going away, and if you bury it, it will only get worse. Take it to God today. As I mentioned, family, friends, and support systems are part of your healing. You don't need many people, even just one or two, and sometimes a wise counselor can help you process your journey.

- Be honest and vulnerable.

  It is surprising how we can hold back on God. It's almost as if we think God doesn't know what we are going through. It can be difficult to express emotion in the form of disappointment, hurt, and anger to God, but he already knows. Honesty and vulnerability help bring healing. Don't think of it as whining or complaining. Yes, there may be others with larger hurts and troubles, but yours are real, and they count. God wants you whole so you can comfort others.

- Pursue healing, but give space for time.

  I'm often surprised by my own foolishness when I delay in taking something to God, and then when I do, I want him to fix it immediately. The desire for personal wholeness and health is good, but it takes time. Lean in with the anticipation of healing, but give it time. The best measure is simply asking, "Am I making progress?"

Reflection: Is there anything in the past or present that you need to take to God today? What is holding you back?

Notes:

SEE THE REAL BATTLE

> Finally, be strong in the Lord and in his mighty power. Put on the full armor of God, so that you can take your stand against the devil's schemes. For our struggle is not against flesh and blood, but against the rulers, against the authorities, against the powers of this dark world and against the spiritual forces of evil in the heavenly realms. Therefore put on the full armor of God, so that when the day of evil comes, you may be able to stand your ground, and after you have done everything, to stand. Stand firm then, with the belt of truth buckled around your waist, with the breastplate of righteousness in place, and with your feet fitted with the readiness that comes from the gospel of peace. In addition to all this, take up the shield of faith, with which you can extinguish all the flaming arrows of the evil one. Take the helmet of salvation and the sword of the Spirit, which is the word of God. And pray in the Spirit on all occasions with all kinds of prayers and requests. With this in mind, be alert and always keep on praying for all the Lord's people.
>
> —Ephesians 6:10–18

Issues such as relational conflict, financial pressures, and strategic alignment can consume us on a daily basis, reminding us that we do have an enemy, and our war against him is indeed real. This daily leadership struggle makes it easy to focus on the temporal challenges happening around us. However, the real battle is connected to the clash of spiritual power in the heavenly realms, where the spiritual forces of good and evil are at war.

Spiritual battle is a daily reality. But for me, there are three to five times a year when the battle is so intense it's truly terrifying.

It's always at night in the early hours, around 2 to 3 a.m. It's always connected to something significant and sometimes personal, but often it's about a bold move for God the church is about to make. I can sense a presence in the room, and my heart starts racing. Sometimes I get up and walk up and down the hallway, praying fervently. Other times I'll grab Patti's hand, wake her, and we pray together. Declaring Jesus's name out loud, we command the forces of evil to leave. Then we claim Jesus's blood having already won the battle. Sometimes it's over soon; sometimes it lasts so long we're exhausted.

You may experience spiritual battles differently, but none of us can take new territory without the enemy fighting back. The good news is that God's presence and power are not only with us, but he has given us spiritual armor for our protection. Without it, I don't think we could stand our ground.

Each piece of the armor is critical and thoroughly prepares and protects us from head to toe. But the scripture for this devotion doesn't stop with the defense of protection. It closes out with an offensive strategy to take up the sword of truth in God's Word and pray in the Spirit.

Evangelical Christians have varied beliefs about the prevalence of spiritual warfare in our modern world. But we can avoid unnecessary theological arguments by agreeing that we do have an enemy, and prayer is a common ground on which we all fight our battles.

Here are several common-ground tactics for prayer:

- Praying in Jesus's name (John 14:14)
- Declaring that you belong to Jesus (Ephesians 1:5)
- Praying by the power of the blood of Jesus (Hebrews 10:19–22)
- Praying by faith (Ephesians 3:12)
- Praying with two or more people (Matthew 18:19)

- Reading or quoting scripture (1 John 5:14)
- Praying for the will of God and about his kingdom (Matthew 6:33)

What new spiritual territory do you hope to take? What are you doing in ministry that the enemy does not like? Do you have others praying with you? Now allow me to be more bold. Are your prayers a comfortable routine, or do they actually recognize and respond to the battle happening around you? Do your prayers confront the enemy who wants to shut down what you are doing for the cause of Christ? These may not be your daily prayers but consider where they fit in your overall prayer life.

Reflection: In what ways might you expand your prayer life to be more proactive in the spiritual battle?

Notes:

EMBRACE BOLD LEADERSHIP

> " After they prayed, the place where they were meeting was shaken. And they were all filled with the Holy Spirit and spoke the word of God boldly.
> —Acts 4:31

I n light of Acts 4:31, I've given thought over the years to the importance of speaking the Word of God boldly. My personality tends to be driven, high-energy, and passionate about progress but not necessarily bold, so being bold requires intentionality for me.

Boldness is not about being loud, having a must-win attitude, or lacking prudence in risk-taking and decision-making. Rather, I think true boldness is always strong but often demonstrates itself through attributes such as humility, kindness, and compassion.

The idea of this verse is not limited to the act of preaching or teaching. The larger context speaks to bold leadership in general. In fact, godly boldness exists before preaching. Boldness is something internal. It must be in you to be authentic, or your words, whether in a Sunday sermon or a boardroom, may sound strong but ring hollow.

I have met church bullies who are bold, but they are not strong in the ways that matter. They may be loud and even passionate about their opinions, but that is obviously not the aim of this scripture. One church bully was a wealthy board member. The church was raising capital for a new building and was excited about some more modern touches, specifically having chairs instead of pews. When the church board member heard about this, he threatened to pull his sizable pledge if the other board members didn't commit to pews. His demand was bold, but his motive was not from the Holy Spirit.

Boldness is also not about personality. When we consider the wide variety of spiritual leaders, the diversity among their personalities is significant. But as the passage for today indicates, they can lead with boldness because they are full of the Holy Spirit. From the more subdued personalities to the more outgoing personalities, they all possess a boldness that clearly originates with the Spirit of God.

Would you say your own personality is more naturally passionate or reserved? I believe that the boldness we seek from the Holy Spirit is not confined to a certain human script. It shows itself through your leadership according to the needs of the kingdom in that moment. And it varies based on what God wants to do in you to shape you for the calling and purpose he has for you.

However, there are common ways to see and sense the power of the Holy Spirit at work in and through your leadership.

Expressions of godly boldness:

- Strength under pressure
  The pressure you carry is like a weight on your shoulders. The higher you rise in leadership, the shorter the list of your responsibilities, but the heavier the weight of those responsibilities. I'm sure you've experienced days or seasons when the weight seemed almost too much to bear. Ask the Holy Spirit to bring strength in those moments to create peace over panic and clarity over confusion. One of the most practical expressions is in decision-making. The strength you receive gives you the boldness required to make tough decisions with clarity under pressure.

- Speaking up in conflict or opposition
  Boldness in a critical meeting or a crucial conversation is frequently required of you as a leader. Your ability to say

what you really think and believe is best is essential. When there is conflict or you face opposition, boldness is needed all the more. This is where the Holy Spirit's power helps you. Prayer is the foundation of your boldness. How are you doing with these conversations?

- Teaching truth with confidence
  I recently listened to two communicators teach biblical and practical sermons on the Holy Spirit to crowds that would not normally be accustomed to that topic and were likely to feel somewhat uncomfortable. Both pastors took a risk and exhibited boldness from scripture rather than from their own personalities or wirings. This inspired their confidence to share the truth. As you reflect on your own teaching, are you as bold as you believe God wants you to be in the settings he gives you?

Reflection: What prevents you from being bold in critical moments? How can you appropriate the Holy Spirit's power to help you?

Notes:

WORSHIP WELL

> Come, let us bow down in worship, let us kneel before the LORD our Maker; for he is our God and we are the people of his pasture, the flock under his care.
>
> —Psalm 95:6–7

Worship may be more private and internal for you, or perhaps you are more outward and demonstrative in your expression of praise. There are times when you may be moved to stand, raise your hands, and jump for joy. Other times you may be quiet, reverent, and awestruck in complete silence before our great God.

True worship is pleasing to God no matter your preferred style. It's not *how* you worship, it's *who* you worship. My hope is that you experience freedom in how you worship but are very clear about who you worship.

One of the deep challenges we must fight against when it comes to who we worship is making sure we overcome our unintentional, default tendency to put ourselves first instead of God. It started in the garden, when Adam and Eve decided to play God. Then it transferred to all of us. God's authority was challenged the moment Satan contradicted God when he told Eve, "You will not certainly die" (Genesis 3:4). As a result, it's part of our natures to challenge authority, rebel, and disobey.

It's not sinful to satisfy God-given natural desires for hunger, sex, companionship, possessions, wisdom, success, and things that are "pleasing to the eye" (Genesis 2:9) in the proper context. It is sinful, however, when we make the choice not to satisfy those desires according to God's commandments. In the garden, Adam and Eve both responded to the challenge before them with defiant arrogance by replacing God with self. Essentially they were saying, like it's possible for any leader to do, "I will do what I want, and I will do it my way" (Genesis 3:6). They decided to satisfy their desires in the way they wanted to rather than to obey God and trust that his ways were better. That's the big question regarding the subject of our worship. Who will be God?

Another practical element is how we worship. I'm a little more reserved in public worship than in my private worship. In my prayer room, I find it most natural to stand when I worship and pray, sometimes with arms raised in awe of God's majesty. That doesn't make it the right way for you to do it; it simply means that's how my soul best connects with God's Spirit in that setting. At other times I intentionally kneel as a physical demonstration of my worship. And sometimes God breaks me when I'm just quietly sitting before him. The point is having freedom in worship. What works for you?

> For the LORD is the great God, the great King above all gods. In his hand are the depths of the earth, and the mountain peaks belong to him. The sea is his, for he made it, and his hands formed the dry land. (Psalm 95:3–5)

God is worthy of our worship. Here are some practical helps for worshipping well:

- Remain clear on who God is.
  God is beyond our comprehension, yet he makes himself real through the beauty of creation and the example of the life of his Son, Jesus. God tells his story in scripture, and all of scripture is a grand revelation of who he is.

Reading about these profound truths can be overwhelming. God's extraordinary love for us allowed him to give his Son, Jesus, in exchange for our sins.

God's grace, forgiveness, and mercy are captivating. How can we resist? When we meditate on the truth of God's redemptive story, what response is there but worship?

- Don't make it complicated.
As a leader I find teaching on the subject of worship or leading the way with worship to be intimidating. But that's probably because I get in the way. If I'm self-conscience or in any way more focused on me than God, I've missed the point.

Worship is simple. Focus on who God is, and declare your love, praise, and gratitude directly to him.

You can worship God for his incredible attributes. He is infinite, eternal, omnipotent, sovereign, holy, faithful, good, loving, merciful, and just. You can praise God for the very breath in your lungs and the health in your body. You can thank God for every good and perfect gift in your life.

Let's take this up a notch. Ask yourself if you worship God when things in your life and ministry aren't going well. That's a tough question. We know we should worship perhaps even more in the challenging times, but emotions like deep disappointment, despair, frustration, and hurt can shut down our worship. One good way to reconnect is to remember who God is, what he's done for you, and that he is always with you.

Reflection: In just a few words, how would you describe your encounters with God when you worship him?

Notes:

PRIORITIZE YOUR FIRST LOVE

> Jesus replied: "Love the Lord your God with all your heart and with all your soul and with all your mind. This is the first and greatest commandment. And the second is like it: Love your neighbor as yourself."
>
> —Matthew 22:37–39

One of my most prized possessions is my dad's army Bible. My parents divorced when I was in elementary school, and I never saw my dad again after the age of ten. I have a couple of pictures, a few letters, and a little brown pocket New Testament of his from the Korean War when he was twenty years old. The cover has *New Testament U.S. Army* imprinted on it. Inside, his handwriting says, "Marvin Reiland, Route #1 Stillwater, Minn., Jan 21, 1951. Hvy. Mortar Co. 135th Infantry, 47th Division," along with his serial number.

I love that little Bible more than you know because it ties me to my dad. We all have something special we love. But when love moves from something to someone, things change. There's a depth and dimension that wasn't there before. When you consider your love for your parents or your spouse and kids, it's something entirely different from your favorite pair of jeans or your most prized family heirloom. It's so much deeper and more meaningful.

There's another even deeper level that scripture calls us to in our love for God. That love is described as one that encompasses all your heart, all your strength, and all your mind. At times I can barely comprehend this, let alone live it. But that is exactly what Jesus said to do.

We love God as we know him. The greater the depth of our relationship connected to our knowledge and experience of God, the greater the potential growth of our love for him. A. W. Tozer wrote, "In Christ and by Christ, God effects complete self-disclosure, although He shows Himself not to reason but to faith and love. Faith is an organ of knowledge, and love an organ of experience."[4]

As leaders, we model love for God. This does not suggest a type of performance but instead, something very real, beautiful, flawed, and yet still powerful and intimate. God's love and our love for him and others is the foundation of our leadership and ministries.

There are three components that help cultivate your love for God:

- Desire
  Deepening your desire for God is a good place to start. Cultivate a desire to pursue him, know him, and love him.

  Our lives are filled with desires. Some are good, some are not, and a few are enjoyable but perhaps unimportant—like my turbocharged desire for chocolate chip cookies. I consider them the eighth wonder of the world. God created them, said they were very good, and I agree. You and God can assess whether your desires are righteous and worth pursuing. I'm just suggesting you acknowledge how real and powerful they are.

  Without a desire for God, the fullness of your life as a leader crowds out time for God. Desire makes time.

---

[4] A. W. Tozer, *The Knowledge of the Holy: The Attributes of God: Their Meaning in the Christian Life* (New York: Harper Collins, 1961), 9.

- Time

  There is no substitute for time in conversation with God if you want to cultivate and demonstrate your love for him. This is not based on duty, obligation, works, or a certain number of minutes. It's merely the recognition that intimate relationships require time. And when we invest time the relationship grows, as does our love for him.

  However, like with your spouse, kids, or close friends, without that time the relationship can't flourish. It may even grow stagnant, or your ability to recognize his voice could be diminished. Don't rush your time with him. Enjoy it, and savor it like an incredible cup of coffee or tea. As each sip is to be experienced, take in each moment with God to the fullest.

- Obedience

  Jesus was clear when he said in John 14:15, "If you love me, keep my commands." Your obedience to God is not based on performance but your desire to please the one you love.

  Discovering God's voice, seeking his will, and following his prompts will deepen your relationship and increase your love. This isn't something for your to-do list; it's about growing a relationship with him for you to cherish and enjoy.

Reflection: How is your love for God evident in your life? In what ways do others see your love for God?

Notes:

ACCEPT YOUR DIVINE ASSIGNMENT

> Then Jesus came to them and said, "All authority in heaven and on earth has been given to me. Therefore go and make disciples of all nations, baptizing them in the name of the Father and of the Son and of the Holy Spirit, and teaching them to obey everything I have commanded you. And surely I am with you always, to the very end of the age."
>
> —Matthew 28:18–20

The concept of partnering with God can be a difficult one to grasp. However, those of us in Christian leadership know it's a uniquely divine partnership. I can hardly grasp the grandeur of God's desire to partner with *me*. I can only begin to imagine a partnership with any of the great kings and presidents of the world, but those would greatly pale when compared to this role. That might sound a bit over the top but not if you take a moment to truly reflect on a literal partnership with a completely spiritual being, the God of the universe.

All Christians are called to live their lives for Christ, but leadership is a different role that carries greater responsibility and accountability. You have an assignment from God, and Jesus makes it clear. Authority was given to him from the Father, and he gives it to you to share the gospel and make disciples. It's easy to get caught up in the mechanics of ministry and leadership, but the mission is clear.

The apostle Paul shared this same assignment as confirmed in Romans 10:13–14: "'Everyone who calls on the name of the Lord will be saved.' How, then, can they call on the one they have not believed in? And how can they believe in the one of whom they have not heard? And how can they hear without someone preaching to them?"

We can feel overwhelmed by the charge given by Jesus and reiterated by Paul, but I've learned that our assignments are best carried out with joy. That is easier to do when we know the distinctions between God's part and our part of the partnership. Of course it's not an equal partnership, and he doesn't need us to advance the kingdom, but he loves us deeply, invites us to join him, and wants us to do well.

GOD'S PART

Let's start with what's already complete and fully accessible: God has revealed himself in scripture, through creation, and through his son, Jesus. He has also made it plain that we are in a spiritual battle. He has told us who the enemy is, and he has told us the outcome. But we don't get to skip the battle. In fact, it would be so much easier if ministry involved only what we could see and touch, but that would never make sense. It would negate how God has provided for our salvation by the blood of Jesus and why he has equipped us with spiritual armor. It's an amazing partnership in the realm of good and evil. Every word you speak, decision you make and person you help, makes a difference.

In addition to what's already complete, there's a powerful force that's alive, current, and in daily action. God sent the Holy Spirit to guide us and bring wisdom and power to our leadership. I've included the topic of the Holy Spirit in several devotions because it seems like the Spirit is often overlooked in the realm of leadership. That shouldn't be, but unfortunately, it's truer than not. This isn't due to lack of belief but rather to missing out on the fullest provision the Holy Spirit has promised us.

How would you assess the work of the Holy Spirit in your own leadership? Do you fully engage his presence and power in your partnership with God?

YOUR PART

- Stay focused.
  God made the plan clear, but it's so easy to get distracted in the busyness of ministry programming and planning that we "forget" about him for a moment. Remembering him keeps us focused on our assignments.

- Trust God.
  Listen for his voice, and trust that he's with you. I can assure you that he has not backed out of his end of the partnership. Lean into his power, not yours.

- Find joy.
  It's the personal joy of leadership that keeps you going. It's the joy of the Spirit that lifts your heart, keeps your perspective healthy, and allows you to put others first.

Reflection: How would you describe your partnership and assignment from God? Which one of the three previous points do you need to focus on right now?

Notes:

KNOW THAT GOD IS WITH YOU

> And I will ask the Father, and he will give you another advocate to help you and be with you forever—the Spirit of truth. The world cannot accept him, because it neither sees him nor knows him. But you know him, for he lives with you and will be in you.
>
> —John 14:16–17

God did not design us to lead alone or live a Christian life in isolation. Yet even though leaders are often surrounded by people, they regularly confess to feeling alone. Perhaps you, too, experience times of loneliness.

For example, you are responsible to make the final decision knowing that there is significant risk, and your leadership team is not fully aligned. That moment can make you feel alone. You are uncertain about what to do, time is running out, and you need to do something.

Perhaps you have been hurt or even attacked by someone in the church. Maybe you have been abandoned or betrayed, like most of us have at one time or another. As beautiful as the church is when it's healthy and working well, it can be ugly when it's toxic and not functioning as God designed. In these times, it's natural to feel alone.

There are other times when it's not about external circumstances but an issue inside you. You might carry a level of insecurity that causes you to pull back, withdraw, or isolate. No matter what the situation might be, it's important to know and believe that you are not alone because God is with you.

What is your level of confidence in the following thoughts?

- God is with you in spirit.
  Today's passage in John 14 promises another advocate, the Spirit of truth, to help you and be with you forever. Verse 17 says that you know him, that he lives with you, and he will be in you! There is power in his presence. Do you sense it? Take a minute now to reflect on this truth, but especially do so when you feel alone in your leadership.

- God is with you through community.
  Since becoming a Christian decades ago, I have nearly always been in some form of a small group. My experience includes men's groups, couples' groups, the church board as a group, and always a group of prayer partners. I have consistently and strongly sensed God's presence through the community of those who love and care about me. It's nearly overwhelming at times. Their heartfelt prayers, support, and kindness are direct representations of the presence of God and his love. I truly hope you experience the same, and if not, that you will soon.

I read an article a few years ago that said 70 percent of pastors feel lonely and can't identify any close friends.[5] I think leaders struggle to build community because they have bought into the lie that they have to appear put together

---

[5] Philip Wagner, "The Secret Pain of Pastors," *Church Pastors*, September 5, 2018. https://churchleaders.com/pastors/pastor-articles/167379-philip-wagner-secret-pain-of-pastors.html.

because of their positions. The truth is that we can uniquely experience God's grace and care through transparency with others.

- God is with you by promise.
One of my favorite Old Testament stories is about Moses's leadership and God's promise that he would be with him. This passage reflects part of the conversation at the burning bush between God and Moses, when God said he saw the suffering of his people and wanted to rescue them from the Egyptians. In Exodus 3:11–12, Moses said to God, "Who am I that I should go to Pharaoh and bring the Israelites out of Egypt?" And God said, "I will be with you. And this will be the sign to you that it is I who have sent you: When you have brought the people out of Egypt, you will worship God on this mountain."

God reminded Moses of his promise again in Exodus 33:12–14, when Moses said to the LORD,

> "You have been telling me, 'Lead these people,' but you have not let me know whom you will send with me. You have said, 'I know you by name and you have found favor with me.' If you are pleased with me, teach me your ways so I may know you and continue to find favor with you. Remember that this nation is your people." The LORD replied, "My Presence will go with you, and I will give you rest."

God kept his promise to Moses and will always keep it with you as well.

Reflection: Which of the above three points do you need to focus on to have a greater sense that God is with you? What will you do to set that in motion this week?

Notes:

EXPERIENCE THE FAITHFULNESS OF GOD

> I will sing of the LORD's great love forever; with my mouth I will make your faithfulness known through all generations. I will declare that your love stands firm forever, that you have established your faithfulness in heaven itself. You said, "I have made a covenant with my chosen one, I have sworn to David my servant, I will establish your line forever and make your throne firm through all generations." The heavens praise your wonders, LORD, your faithfulness too, in the assembly of the holy ones. For who in the skies above can compare with the LORD? Who is like the LORD among the heavenly beings? In the council of the holy ones God is greatly feared; he is more awesome than all who surround him. Who is like you, LORD God Almighty? You, LORD, are mighty, and your faithfulness surrounds you.
>
> —Psalm 89:1–8

Three times the psalmist asks the rhetorical question, "Who is like the LORD?" The inferred response is unquestionably, no one! God's love is so great, so extravagant, and so faithful!

The great I Am, Creator of the heavens and earth and all that is in it, is faithful in his love for you. The loving Father who created humankind to share an intimate and personal relationship with him established a covenant for all generations! God's faithful loving-kindness is so great that his covenant promise provided a way for eternal life through his Son, Jesus. Take a moment to praise and thank him!

Here are three ways to experience the faithfulness of God:

- Rest in weary times.
  There's an old saying that says, "The church never sleeps." My hunch is that you immediately connect with what that means. In forty years of church leadership, I've never finished my to-do list. How about you? There is always another person to connect with, problem to solve, meeting to go to, and lesson to write. I love every minute of it, but it can be exhausting. Can you relate?

  When I reflect on this passage of God's faithfulness, unending love, and majesty of his holiness, I find rest at a soul level. I know he is with me and lifts me up. He's there for you as well.

- Delight in the good times.
  We can delight in God at all times, but it's good to remember God when things are going well. It's easy to get comfortable when pressure is low and most things are up and to the right. It's in those times that both the small and large blessings deserve our delight in God.

  We can literally pause for a few seconds anytime during the day and thank him for his goodness and the specific blessing. This cultivates a generous heart and helps keep us focused on the true source of all that is good.

- Trust in tough times.
  Do you remember March 2020, when the COVID-19 pandemic led to drastic changes in where we could go and what we could do? Who could forget, right? That was the

first time in our lifetimes that churches closed their physical buildings for worship services. It was an unsettling time, but it's in times like those we all quickly understand the need to trust in God's faithfulness.

We don't trust God because we have no choice. We trust him because he is faithful and won't let us down.

Here are three ways to participate in God's faithfulness:

- Communicate God's love.
  One of the greatest gifts you can give anyone is to communicate verbally the love of God. God's love is the foundational gift in his faithfulness. Humanly, we comprehend love more in conditional terms, and when those terms are broken, love ends. But God's love is unconditional. Unconditional love is radical and transformational.

  Over and over again remind those you serve that God loves them no matter what. Even the skeptics will lean in when they hear this truth.

- Demonstrate God's love.
  We can demonstrate God's love in so many ways, such as grace, kindness, forgiveness, truth, sacrifice, generosity, encouragement, and hope. I'm sure you could add several more to the list.

  As God faithfully pours his love out upon you, it's your great privilege to pass it on to others. My hope is that it doesn't seem like a task but like something more from the overflow. The hope is that for all of us, this becomes a natural part our lives. It's not a competition, and it may be as small as letting someone go in front you in line at the grocery store or as grand as something I recently heard about when a friend gave another friend a kidney!

- Lead with God's love.
  Authority, decision-making, and your leadership in general change dramatically by how much they are guided by the love of God. We tend to give more grace, serve more joyfully, and sacrifice without complaint when God's love is leading.

  Through the lens of God's love, authority is seen as responsibility not power, decision-making is viewed as a matter of stewardship, and influence is used for the good of others.

Reflection: What is God teaching you today about his faithfulness and how to participate in it as a leader?

Notes:

PREVENT BURNOUT

> Let us not become weary in doing good, for at the proper time we will reap a harvest if we do not give up.
>
> —Galatians 6:9

nother friend just threw in the towel. He's out of ministry. As I think about his story of burnout, as with every similar story I hear, I wonder if it could have been prevented.

What I'm learning is that every story is very different, but we tend to lump them all in the generic category of, "They just worked too much." My friend did work hard but would tell you he didn't work too much. There was so much more to his story. He was an associate pastor who didn't feel appreciated, and whose church wasn't doing well in general. In addition, his family life was stressful because his personal finances caused increasing pressure.

Was burnout preventable? I don't know for sure, but I believe the answer has to be yes, or we'd all burn out and throw in the towel eventually. Of course, burnout isn't the only reason a leader might quit ministry, but it's a very common reason and, therefore, the focus of this devotion.

His situation, like most, didn't happen overnight. It was a long, slow simmer that finally turned to a boil; by then it was too late. When the water gets that hot, you've got to get out or get hurt. Unfortunately, you never get out completely unscathed. And it can take a lot of time and therapy to get back to health and productivity after burnout.

One of the keys to preventing burnout is early detection. We may not see it coming or be able to get ahead of it unless we regularly self-assess and get real about the elements of our lives that are leading us down its path.

Quiet and honest reflection on these five questions will serve you well in the prevention of burnout if you take action on areas that need improvement:

- Are you working too many hours?
  Start with getting honest about how many hours you actually work. This doesn't include the hours spent at the gym, a dentist appointment, or a school event with your kids. Then compare that to the number of hours you think is healthy for you. If you are working too much, the first step is to set boundaries. For example, establish the time you need to go home each day and how many nights out each week is right for you.

- What is your work environment like?
  What's it like where you work? Do you feel appreciated? Are you being developed? Do you enjoy the people you work with? These things matter and play a huge factor in the kind of stress that leads to burnout. When an environment is positive, caring, and healthy, working hard is enjoyable and invigorating. If your environment is not as healthy and lifegiving as needed, what could you do to change it?

- What is your home life like?
  It's possible that a leader doesn't work too many hours and the church environment is healthy, but his or her life at home is tense and filled with friction. How about you? Does your home life contribute to or help prevent burnout? The good news is you can change the course and condition of your family life. If you need help, don't hesitate to reach out. Talk to a trusted friend, mentor, or counselor.

- Are your calling, position, and passion aligned?

  Most church leaders wouldn't say they hate their jobs, but an alarming number don't believe they're in the right position that fits their callings, talents, and passions. How about you? Are you in the right seat on the bus? There are no perfect seats, but there is one that will seem to please God, fit you, and benefit the church.

- Are you taking care of yourself physically?

  You may not want to think about your diet and exercise, but they have to be on this list. They're vitally important. Regular exercise and smart eating go a long way to fostering a healthy ministry. You don't have to flip tires and drink something green and slimy for breakfast. You can even eat a doughnut on occasion! It's the three doughnuts with four cups of coffee to wash them down, followed by wings and fries later that are the problem.

As you consider all this, remember this is a lifelong process, and you shouldn't try to do it all alone. Seek help and accountability to make it for the long haul and not be tempted to give up. You'll reap a harvest in time.

Reflection: Which of these five questions do you need start with, and what is your first step?

Notes:

RELISH SOUL-LEVEL REST

> "Come to me, all you who are weary and burdened, and I will give you rest."
>
> —Matthew 11:28

There are different kinds of rest. For example, you can stretch for a few minutes after a long run, you can read a good book on a quiet afternoon, you can chill on your day off, and you can get some good sleep every night. These kinds of rest do a good job taking care of normal everyday fatigue.

Can you recall a time when your work as a leader took you beyond a normal tired?

There have been times when I would describe my weariness as bone-level fatigue. This happens when long days accumulate into weeks or even months of weariness that can't be managed with a power nap or even a few days off. That level of sustained intensity can make you weary to the marrow.

You know what that's like. Maybe you've launched a new campus, navigated a complex and conflict-laden relationship, or opened a new building. It's exhausting. I remember not long ago when I taught about thirteen times in a period of about twenty-one days. Several of the talks were at 12Stone, but the others required travel, all while still caring for my responsibilities as executive pastor/ chief of staff. I have a lot of energy, but I was running on fumes. I landed in one city only to realize that I had left all my notes for those talks in my car at the airport in Atlanta. I panicked! I was ready to call the Pentagon, book *Air Force One*, and summon the national guard. I was desperate to do whatever it took to get those notes. When I connected with my administrative assistant, she calmly asked, "Why don't you just print them out again at the front desk of the hotel?" to which I sheepishly responded, "That's a good idea." I was simply maxed out. The good thing is I recognized it and was able to take some time off.

I recently spoke with a pastor who hadn't taken a day off in months because his church was experiencing terrible internal conflict. The board was upset, a few staff members were leaving, and the congregation would be fully aware of it all soon. A potential church split loomed over a culturally divisive issue. It was a mess, and the burden on the pastor was overwhelming. He was numb.

While these examples highlight the added pressure and stress our work lives can create, our weariness is not limited to the workplace. We can experience weariness from navigating a dysfunctional relationship in our personal lives or from trying to manage a sin issue. Whatever the case may be, the results of weariness are often layered and cumulative. They can include relational heartbreaks, health concerns, consequences of sin or bad decisions, and more.

This kind of weariness needs a different kind of rest—a soul-level rest that will first help you regain your sense of normalcy, and second, sustain a healthy rhythm in your life and ministry.

- If you are weary at a soul level, this invitation from Jesus is for you.

  If you are not experiencing this kind of weariness or heavy burden, that's good, but the invitation is still for you. You are well positioned to *sustain* the soul-level rest Jesus has for you. Be sure to continue a faithful practice of a Sabbath day off because God designed rest into the rhythm of creation.

- The primary difference in the kind of rest is whether it is natural or supernatural.

  You can orchestrate and take care of rest in the natural realm. Only Jesus can give you supernatural rest. He simply says, "Come to me." How remarkable and refreshing that we just need Jesus. There is a power behind his promise that lifts you from what weighs you down. He is asking you to trust that his very presence and power can lift your soul from weary desperation to a place of newness and restoration.

Jesus wants us to exchange our human burdens, yokes of sin, and earthly work for his yoke of simply trusting in him. He has completed the work, and soul rest is a gift. There is no gimmick or five-step process. Rest will come from your connection to Jesus's presence. He is the vine, and you are one of the branches.

Sometimes the situations we face do not disappear in a few days or weeks, but no matter what, Jesus delivers rest.

Reflection: Is there anything that prevents you from trusting the presence of Jesus to bring the soul-level rest you need?

Notes:

BREAK FREE FROM SECRETS

> You have searched me, LORD, and you know me. You know when I sit and when I rise; you perceive my thoughts from afar. You discern my going out and my lying down; you are familiar with all my ways. Before a word is on my tongue you, LORD, know it completely. You hem me in behind and before, and you lay your hand upon me. Such knowledge is too wonderful for me, too lofty for me to attain.
>
> —Psalm 139:1–6

To know and be known is the longing of every human soul, yet we fear being found out. We fear that once we are known, we may not be accepted for who we really are at our deepest core. God's desire for us is that we lay that fear aside and be open in the fullest sense to authentic and meaningful relationships with others. Unfortunately, though, our inclinations to hide creep in through fears and insecurities.

To know and be known starts with you and God. You are made in his likeness. The more you know God the better you'll know yourself; and the more you know yourself, the better you'll know God. That's what relationship offers. It's not merely an issue of knowledge, though that is vital, but also awareness, vulnerability, and authenticity.

Of course a Creator-created relationship is different than human relationships, but the pattern of connection, trust, and exchange exists in both. It's life-changing to know that God *desires* a give-and-take relationship with us. Our relationship with him requires personal interaction. It's not meant to be mechanical; it should be authentic and alive. Each day we make choices that impact the nature of that relationship.

God is familiar with you (Psalm 139:3). You can be yourself. He delights in you as you are. Yes, sin can erode connection and trust, but God provided a way to restore both because he knew ahead of time that would be necessary.

In a small gathering of church leaders a pastor once said, "You are only as sick as your secrets." At first, that was a jolting statement. But as I listened, I gleaned the truth in it. It's what we hide that gets us in trouble. Being fully known and responding to sin in a healthy and responsible way is the path God provides to freedom and maturity.

Your relationship with God is a divine interaction with him through prayer, worship, serving, relationships, and the expressions of your leadership. As a leader, you carry that divine interaction into your daily work. The pattern of knowing and being known has a tremendous impact on your leadership. Let's break that down into three parts:

- Connection
  Your personal connection with God sets the pace for your connection with others. In fact, a heart-level connection with God helps you enjoy the beauty of your relationship with him and others. It also serves as the bedrock for how you lead because if you don't know how to connect, you can't lead. And if your connection with God is weak, you are not likely to follow him very well.

  In a small-group meeting, a frustrated dad opened up about his lack of connection with his teenage son. One of the older and wiser men in the group asked him how well he and his son knew each other, and he got teary. There were no intentional secrets between them, but there was also no effort to know or be known by one another. They had unintentionally kept so much about themselves hidden. As a result of that conversation, this dad realized why he couldn't lead his son well and wasn't enjoying the relationship he wanted. There was no intimate connection.

- Trust
  An authentic heart-level connection also leads to trust, the foundation of all healthy and productive relationships. We often talk about our level of trust in God, but what an intriguing thought to consider whether God can trust us. Am I worthy of God's trust in me over all that he has placed in my hands? How about you?

  That same frustrated dad spoke with the small group about trust. He was honest in saying he didn't trust his son, and that was a barrier to the relationship. Relational trust is a two-way proposition, and he knew he needed to work on trust.

- Exchange
  Relationships are always a two-way street. They are not transactional, but there is an exchange of giving and receiving as each person makes positive investments of value in the other. Neither expects anything in return but is blessed because of the return. This isn't a score-keeping situation, but we all know what it's like to be in a relationship that's a one-way street, where one person does all the giving. A healthy relationship is not designed to be that way.

  Perhaps you've not considered your relationship with God to be a heart-level exchange, but it is. For example, when you pray, he responds. When he speaks, you can obey. The interaction is tangible.

Reflection: In what relationship, including with God, do you need to be more authentic and vulnerable? What is your first step in connecting with someone at the heart level?

Notes:

KEEP YOUR STANDARDS HIGH

> Here is a trustworthy saying: Whoever aspires to be an overseer desires a noble task. Now the overseer is to be above reproach, faithful to his wife, temperate, self-controlled, respectable, hospitable, able to teach, not given to drunkenness, not violent but gentle, not quarrelsome, not a lover of money. He must manage his own family well and see that his children obey him, and he must do so in a manner worthy of full respect. (If anyone does not know how to manage his own family, how can he take care of God's church?) He must not be a recent convert, or he may become conceited and fall under the same judgment as the devil. He must also have a good reputation with outsiders, so that he will not fall into disgrace and into the devil's trap. In the same way, deacons are to be worthy of respect, sincere, not indulging in much wine, and not pursuing dishonest gain. They must keep hold of the deep truths of the faith with a clear conscience. They must first be tested; and then if there is nothing against them, let them serve as deacons.
>
> —1 Timothy 3:1–10

When you read this passage, what is your first thought about the list of standards for leaders? What is your first emotion? When I read this passage, it's easy for me to see how easily I could fall short of the biblical standard of leadership, and this is only one passage of many (also see Titus 1:6–9), but I can't let that be an excuse for me to skip over it. My desire is to rise to the standards without having a sense of performance or pursuing some level of unattainable perfection.

The long list included in this passage can be overwhelming, so I find it helpful to start by simplifying it into categories. I find seven important standards:

- Leadership is a godly calling.
- Leadership is not automatically open to everyone.
- Leaders live a life of integrity and virtue.
- Leaders cultivate a good family life.
- Leaders possess a good attitude.
- Leaders faithfully study God's Word.
- Leaders have the right perspective toward money.

The list is humbling, but because of God's power in us, it is not overwhelming. If we distill it further, the overarching principle is that spiritual leadership is a high calling. And with a high calling comes high standards. This calling is an honor, and the standards reflect the One who calls us.

I remember well my ordination service. From the powerful sermon preached by a Wesleyan general superintendent to the vows I publicly promised to the prayer over Patti and me, it was truly a sacred moment. The standards for ordination are high. I served, studied, and was tested for years to get to that moment. Afterwards, my district superintendent, Steve, came up to me, and shook my hand, and said, "We're so glad you're on the team. Now try really hard not to mess up."

I still smile at that moment. One might question his motivational methods, but he made his expectation clear. Don't mess up. I appreciate that. Now I have to add that if you know Steve, a godly man and good friend to this day, you know he also understands grace. When I did mess up, he was there for me, as was the grace of God.

It's not that any one thing in this passage is complicated or unattainable, but it all takes character. It requires discipline that is filled with joyful obedience. It is not the drudgery of lifeless duty.

It's also not a checklist of hard tasks. Rather, it is a godly standard that is a privilege to pursue. When we miss the mark, we can make it right and keep going.

- If you are struggling, talk to God and a trusted friend.
- If you are thriving, thank God and keep going.
- If another leader is struggling, come alongside and help him or her to rise up.

The leaders I admire most seem to embrace and live out this whole passage through one word—humility. Humble leadership recognizes both our humanity and our responsibilities. Our humanity invites grace but does not dismiss our responsibilities to those we serve and the God who calls us. How would your peers and those you lead assess your humility?

Reflection: According to the list of seven standards, where are you thriving, and where are you struggling? What is the first step you need to take to rise higher?

Notes:

INFLUENCE THROUGH TRUTH

> All Scripture is God-breathed and is useful for teaching, rebuking, correcting and training in righteousness, so that the servant of God may be thoroughly equipped for every good work.
>
> —2 Timothy 3:16–17

The term "fake news" is now embedded in our culture. The concept has always existed, but more recently it has received a name. And while there is validity to the idea that people in positions of influence might propagate their own agendas by circulating fake news stories, the problem is that it's hard to know what is true and what isn't. Confusion comes when what is circulated has elements of truth, but it's not the entire truth.

We need a true north on which to base our leadership, or the subjectivity of nearly every issue we face will result in a descent to confusion or even chaos. On a practical level, without a true north, we spend our time in debate, and nothing gets accomplished. That true north is the Word of God. Seems simple, but it's not. Why?

Typically, we first trust a person before we trust the actual content. That means if we trust the source, we trust the content. But that works for good only when that person bases his or her thinking on the values from an infallible source, the Word of God.

We can see a personal example here as Paul writes to Timothy, "But as for you, continue in what you have learned and have become convinced of, because you know those from whom you learned it, and how from infancy you have known the Holy Scriptures, which are able to make you wise for salvation through faith in Christ Jesus" (2 Timothy 3:14–15). Paul was essentially stating to Timothy that you know and trust those who have taught you, and you know the scriptures are true.

We, too, have the infallible truth of God's Word. It is the foundation upon which we test all other information. It helps us discern to the best of our abilities what is true and good as we lead others. It is our true north. God's Word is our standard and baseline. We also have others who walk closely with God who have led and influenced our abilities to lead well. However, we need to remember that the character of the messenger can affect whether truth is accepted or rejected. That is a huge responsibility for you and me as leaders. It's a significant weight on our shoulders to grasp that whether someone may trust the truth in God's Word depends on who we are as leaders.

I have served with Kevin Myers for twenty years, and I can tell you he's one of the most trustworthy people I know. Time and time again, I've watched him set his own personal agenda or desires aside for the good of the team and the congregation as a whole. And whether he is teaching from scripture on Sunday mornings or casting vision in the boardroom during a meeting, his words carry the authentic ring of truth. This comes from two things: a life immersed in the Word and decades of trustworthy leadership.

Further, in my personal relationship with Kevin, he is strong enough to speak truth and kind enough to offer grace. That combination increases trust. It paints a good picture of what it takes for all of us to lead in truth.

Two practical points for meditation:

- Your love and study of God's Word must be consistent.
  My favorite book in the Bible is Ephesians. My favorite characters are Moses and Nehemiah, and I love to linger in the Psalms. How about you? What are your favorites? The

personal favorites that you return to over and over are great, but all of scripture must be part of your study. New insights from scripture must continually transform you so that you can always lead from a position of authentic truth.

- Your leadership must be trustworthy.
  In Paul's letter to Timothy, he also writes, "Do your best to present yourself to God as one approved, a worker who does not need to be ashamed and who correctly handles the word of truth" (2 Timothy 2:15).

Trustworthy leadership is a lifelong endeavor, and it can be lost in a moment of poor decision. Staying close to God's Word and guarding your heart through prayer is a wise path to follow.

Reflection: How has the Word of God shaped your thinking in the past three months?

Notes:

LEAD YOURSELF FIRST

> Do you not know that in a race all the runners run, but only one gets the prize? Run in such a way as to get the prize. Everyone who competes in the games goes into strict training. They do it to get a crown that will not last, but we do it to get a crown that will last forever. Therefore I do not run like someone running aimlessly; I do not fight like a boxer beating the air. No, I strike a blow to my body and make it my slave so that after I have preached to others, I myself will not be disqualified for the prize.
> —1 Corinthians 9:24–27

Before you can lead others well, you must first lead yourself. And if you are like me, you may be the most difficult person you lead. Do you ever disagree with yourself only then to change your mind? How about the thing you promised yourself you wouldn't do, but you did it anyway?

God and I have been in a lengthy dispute about fasting. It's not a command, but Matthew 6:16–17 says, "when" you fast. These verses capture my attention. Fasting has been part of my spiritual life, but for some reason, I've faltered for a while now in practicing it regularly. When prompted by the Holy Spirit, I fast for a few meals here and there, maybe a day, but it feels like I miss the mark. It's strange really, that I can often get so wrapped up in my work that I miss lunch and even forget dinner. No big deal! But when I tell myself to fast, I'm like a crazed person who will attack for a five-day-old doughnut.

How about you? What area of self-leadership do you need to

strengthen? Before you get too deeply into that answer, let's look at three factors necessary for successful self-leadership.

- Motivation
  The why, or the reason, for your desired behavior will often determine the level of your success. If you want it badly enough, you'll make the sacrifice. This will help you love and serve God more deeply.

- Discipline
  The apostle Paul makes it clear in our passage from 1 Corinthians that discipline is required for self-leadership and to remain qualified to lead. He paints vivid pictures like a runner going in circles or a boxer punching the sky to illustrate someone without discipline.

- Character
  You've heard it said that integrity, or good character, is about doing the right thing even when no one is looking. I've heard it said that you can tell a lot about someone's character by whether or not they return the shopping cart at the grocery store. It's often the little things that reveal the big issues. For leaders, character involves living the same life you expect of others.

Here are a few areas to consider when it comes to your self-leadership. Keep in mind the focus of your self-leadership is for God's glory and should be motivated by your love for him.

- Self-leadership in your spiritual life
  The fact that you are reading this devotional is a good indicator of self-leadership in your spiritual life. Keep going. From your prayer life to your thought life, is God prompting you to work on a certain discipline?

- Self-leadership in your physical life
  Exercise requires discipline, but the results are worth it. Even if you just take a brisk walk several times a week, positive results will be created. As for eating habits, well none of us needs a lecture, so let me simply encourage you to eat wisely.

- Self-leadership in your social and family lives
  Few things are more important than your relationships. A big-picture overview would include managing your emotions, giving more than you take, and serving your friends and family well. This is a lifetime endeavor!

- Self-leadership in your professional life
  No matter how accomplished we become as leaders, there are always ways we can improve if we seek them out. Perhaps there is a professional advancement course you could take advantage of, some books and podcasts you may need to add to your growth plan this year, or maybe even a leadership coach or mentor. But always keep in mind your growth as a leader is always for God's glory (Colossians 3:17).

Please don't be too tough on yourself if you have several areas you want to improve. Committing to growth-oriented change and making steady progress is the goal. Ask God to help you in one area at a time, and consider giving someone in your life permission to walk alongside you for accountability and encouragement. It's as you submit yourself to God and continue to grow in your ability to lead yourself that he can use you to coach and equip those you lead.

Reflection: Is there something you need to start or stop? What area of self-leadership do you sense the Holy Spirit is prompting you to strengthen first?

Notes:

FIGHT FOR PURITY

> How can a young person stay on the path of purity? By living according to your word. I seek you with all my heart; do not let me stray from your commands. I have hidden your word in my heart that I might not sin against you. Praise be to you, LORD; teach me your decrees. With my lips I recount all the laws that come from your mouth. I rejoice in following your statutes as one rejoices in great riches. I meditate on your precepts and consider your ways. I delight in your decrees; I will not neglect your word.
>
> —Psalm 119:9–16

I t's one thing to remain pure for a moment or a day or two; it's wholly another thing to stay pure over the course of a lifetime. In fact, it's humanly impossible without the truth and power of God's Word and forgiveness of sin. I suspect the psalmist in today's passage started with a question about how a person can stay on a path of purity simply because it's universally challenging to navigate.

The intent of this psalm is likely meant to be broader in nature than just sexual sin, but we'll focus on physical purity because it's such a dominant part of the human struggle, and candidly, because so many leaders fall from sexual sin.

My heart breaks because far too many of my colleagues and even a few friends are no longer leading in a church because of this issue. None of us is above sexual temptation. Don't let the enemy whisper to you, "It can't happen to you." Perhaps it's not likely, but the moment you think, *Not me*, is the moment you are more susceptible.

Sadly, the enemy tempts many church leaders to say yes to the wrong desires. And for the sake of their sins, they often walked away from great ministries, beautiful families, and the promise of impacting many more lives for Jesus. Let me be clear, these are veteran leaders who are gifted, smart, and have served very well. But they made the foolish choice to pursue someone other than their spouses. And the irony is that they have likely counseled many other leaders not to do what they ended up doing themselves. Needless to say, none of us is above the tactics of the enemy of our souls, so we need to stay strong and alert. Here are three guidelines to help you:

- Set your heart on the right desire.
  The path to purity begins with wanting purity more than impurity. Most Christian leaders desire and pursue sexual purity, but that alone is not enough. You have to acknowledge the lure and desire of impurity. This means it's vital that you acknowledge that what is sexually impure is alluring and enticing. You must resist, or temptation will win.

  Consider this common scenario. You experience a connection with someone of the opposite sex. It may even be a genuine spiritual connection related to a shared purpose in ministry. You notice the energy and chemistry, and you enjoy it because, after all, you are serving God together. Left unresisted, however, that connection can lead to attraction, which makes it easy to engage in innocent touches, lingering glances, long hours together, or perhaps even occasionally time spent alone. Ultimately, the attraction leads to temptation, and the temptation might lead to sin. The way to resist begins by desiring purity more.

- Meditate on God's Word.
  The writer of Psalm 119 repeatedly draws your attention to making every effort to live your life according to God's Word.

Committing to God's commands, depositing his Word within your heart and mind, declaring his laws, following his statutes, delighting in his decrees, and not neglecting his Word create a safeguard against sin.

There is power in reading, knowing, understanding, internalizing, meditating, and memorizing scripture because the Holy Spirit can use those disciplines to strengthen you and help you escape temptation. In fact, scripture is your primary tool toward purity because it helps align your heart and mind with the heart and mind of God.

- Set up your fences.
Fences are generally known for preventing us from going places we should not go. It's a simple image that works well for such a complex process.

It's easy to say, "Just don't," or to say to yourself, "I won't." But those words of self-determination break down over time with fatigue, pressure, and a diet of less prayer and scripture than you need. These fences will serve you well in remaining on the path of purity:

Fence 1: Fortify your mind and willpower with scripture.

Make it a practice to know God's standards, strengthen your mind, and develop your willpower through scripture, so you can know the lines you won't cross.

Fence 2: Know when you are on the warning track.

In the outfield of every baseball field there is a warning track that helps the player know when he is getting close to the wall. Typical warning tracks for you may include flirtation, what you look at on social media, and what thoughts you dwell on.

Fence 3: Drop your coat and run.

You know the story of Joseph and Potiphar's wife. She caught him by his cloak and invited him to go to bed with her. But he left his cloak in her hand and ran out of the house (Genesis 39:12). If the first two fences have not stopped you, and you are face-to-face with a big mistake, run.

Reflection: How will you fortify your fences?

Notes:

STRIVE TO WILLINGLY FOLLOW

> Then he said to them all: "Whoever wants to be my disciple must deny themselves and take up their cross daily and follow me. For whoever wants to save their life will lose it, but whoever loses their life for me will save it."
>
> —Luke 9:23–24

Jesus calls us all to follow. It's difficult to lead well if we can't follow well.

For many years Patti wanted us to take ballroom dance lessons. I asked her why, and she quickly and confidently answered, "So I can wear a beautiful ballroom dress!" I told her I would love to be with the beautiful girl in the new dress, so off we went, and I tried not to look too goofy.

During the lessons, I learned that one person always leads, and the other always follows. It only works if you have one of each, and they both need to be good at their respective roles. A good leader and a bad follower equals trouble. A good follower and a bad leader also equals trouble.

As it turns out, "It takes two to tango," is a leadership principle.

We learn followership as we follow God's leadership through submission to the precepts and commands he outlines in his Word and through listening to God in prayer and obeying him when he directs us. But this also translates into our human experiences. For example, a senior pastor demonstrates followership by submitting to a decision from the church board or a denominational official. A staff member follows his or her supervisor by fulfilling agreed-upon responsibilities. In the same way, a volunteer leader follows a staff member's direction.

Followership is a choice; no one is forced to follow. That's part of the beauty and power of your willingness to follow. When you choose to say yes to a job or a volunteer role, you choose to follow. Followership is also an attitude that is based on character, and humility is the core character trait of a follower's attitude. If you often resist or resent following your leaders, it's important to take time in reflection to ask yourself why.

Many people, particularly inexperienced leaders, function under the notion that leadership means you do the leading, not the following. Keep in mind, however, that an unwillingness to follow doesn't necessarily make you a visionary, a trendsetter, or an entrepreneur. And a healthy view of followership does not include a complete surrender and death to everything you think, your opinions, or your desires.

Jesus models followership with the Father:

> Jesus gave them this answer: "Very truly I tell you, the Son can do nothing by himself; he can do only what he sees his Father doing, because whatever the Father does the Son also does." (John 5:19)

> "By myself I can do nothing; I judge only as I hear, and my judgment is just, for I seek not to please myself but him who sent me." (John 5:30)

> "For even the Son of Man did not come to be served, but to serve, and to give his life as a ransom for many." (Mark 10:45)

A willing spirit of submission is the foundation of followership:

- Submission prevents a spirit of rebellion.
  No one teaches a two-year-old to say no. It's already in him or her. Rebellion is in our spiritual DNA. (See Genesis chapter 3.) Rebellion within our souls leads to discontentment, which often leads to conflict and division rather than unity and progress. The continual practice of surrendering our wills earns greater spiritual authority.

- Submission prevents a spirit of arrogance.
  Arrogance is the opposite of humility. It's at the core of pride, overconfidence, and self-importance. None of us escapes the potential for arrogance, but we can all resist the temptation. Rarely does a leader move from humble submission directly to egotistical arrogance. It's a slow slide. Catch it early and arrest it.

- Submission prevents a spirit of independence.
  The nuance here is subtle because there is a healthy aspect to independence. We raise our kids to a mature sense of independence to go out and live successfully on their own. However, an immature sense of independence is to believe you don't need anyone and prefer to do it all your way. Mature submission recognizes the need for interdependence and healthy relationships.

Leadership truly is a dance that includes both leading and following. The secret is to learn the right rhythm of when to step forward and when to step back.

Reflection: What practical demonstration of followership would you most want to see in those who follow you? Does your leadership model that example?

Notes:

WATCH THE TONE OF YOUR LEADERSHIP

> So in everything, do to others what you would have them do to you, for this sums up the Law and the Prophets.
>
> —Matthew 7:12

I can remember more than once as a kid my mom saying to me, "I don't like the tone of your voice." Those were never fun moments. I was probably arguing or being disrespectful. I learned at an early age that a great deal of life is lived in the nuances, and it's not just what you say in those moments but how you say it. Tone matters, and how you treat people sets the tone of your leadership.

The tone of your leadership is evident to all those you serve. How would others describe your tone? Is there an edge? Do you communicate joy? Do you show that you love to serve? Does your tone change based on the daily pressures of leadership?

Understanding your tone will help ensure that you don't unintentionally or carelessly treat people poorly. But we all have blind spots. We can't see what we can't see. Pressure can build to the point that we sometimes carry a low-grade angst rather than peace and poise. When this happens, people can often sense how we feel about them even when we aren't saying anything or asking anything of them.

Consider these three ways to treat people that always have a positive impact:

- Kindness
It is unlikely you'll ever see a workshop at a leadership conference on the topic of kindness. We don't often talk about kindness in leadership circles, at least not in terms of what is required to be an effective leader. We focus more on drive, tough-mindedness, decision-making, and progress. Rightfully so because those are important attributes. But they don't make a longstanding difference if there is an accompanying shortage of kindness.

    Kindness is an essential human quality that allows trust, connection, and genuine exchange to take place. Kindness brings peace and joy into pressure-filled situations. Most important, kindness is a fruit of the Holy Spirit that pleases God. Accordingly, we can ask him to help us develop that attribute more fully in our relationships with others.

    Kindness embodies genuine humility because it embraces the idea of thinking about others before yourself. Kindness carries a desire to serve others with joy, and it requires taking the initiative and expecting nothing in return. Kindness requires personal security and contentment because if you are insecure or lack inner contentment, it's difficult to focus on others.

- Respect
Respect is shown in small everyday ways that result in big impacts. Our senior pastor, Kevin, has always treated me with respect. One way that has meant so much to me is that he asks about my calendar and what would work best for my schedule as we plan meetings. Kevin could exercise his privilege of being my boss and simply tell me to be at a meeting, but only in rare circumstances, usually beyond his control, does that happen.

In fact, he often gives me a choice of my preference and goes with my choice! That communication of respect for my time and energy has had a huge impact on me.

Respect can be demonstrated for others' opinions, their experiences, and for who they are as individuals. The easiest way to think about this is to consider how you want others to show respect to you, and then do the same for them.

- Grace
Perhaps the greatest gift we can receive is to be forgiven when we wrong someone. To forgive others extends that gift.

One of the tones of grace is to extend it before an offense is made. That means to give the benefit of the doubt. From emails and texts to something said in haste at a meeting, it's amazing how much good believing the best and giving the benefit of the doubt will do. Sometimes just pausing and counting to five before you respond can mean the difference between grace and a relational disaster.

God has lavished grace on you and desires that you generously give it to others as well. Grace and truth are often combined because they provide a biblical balance. But when it comes to how you treat people, it's rare that you will take grace too far.

Reflection: Of kindness, respect, and grace, which one do you need to focus on most right now? What is your first step?

Notes:

EMBODY COACHABLE LEADERSHIP

" Let a righteous man strike me—that is a kindness; let him rebuke me—
that is oil on my head. My head will not refuse it, for my prayer will still
be against the deeds of evildoers.

—Psalm 141:5

Proverbs 27:6 echoes this not-quickly-embraced-but-important principle: "Wounds from a friend can be trusted, but an enemy multiplies kisses." A brief hurt from someone you trust can protect you from long-term pain. And in the same way, a teachable spirit goes a long way in your walk with God and your leadership among those you serve.

Do you know someone who has difficulty owning a mistake or taking responsibility for a problem he or she caused? If that's a pattern, it will be difficult for people to get close to, connect with, or even respect that person. If the person is a leader, it will cause serious problems over time.

When I was a teenager, it really made me mad when my parents would correct me. It was especially irritating when it was about schoolwork, friends, or dating. I was an immature teenager then, so I thought I knew more than they did. It's embarrassing to look back at it now, but I'm glad to say I've grown up a lot since then.

Now I'm deeply grateful for wise and godly people who call me out on something they see that I should change. I know that's one of the keys to accelerating my growth. How about you? How receptive are you to holy reproof from a trusted friend, coach, or boss? Correction is a holy gift when it comes from a heart of love, and it ultimately advances the gospel because it makes me a better leader.

Why would a leader reject reproof? It happens surprisingly frequently. I've already mentioned immaturity being a big reason for its rejection. A few other common reasons are insecurities, pride, and a lack of self-awareness that prevent them from seeing the truth.

But let's give a little more grace. It can also be because they have been deeply hurt, and the rejection is simply a natural defense mechanism. Or it could be because they are truly exhausted and have no margin to absorb it. Or sometimes it's because they don't have enough experience with healthy and close relationships to know how to trust and receive corrections.

No matter the reason, rejecting constructive criticism is an unwise choice. The following are some benefits of your receptivity to correction.

- It's how you grow.
  We all enjoy a party, vacation, and taking a little break, but you don't grow in those situations. It's in the times of facing challenges, digging deep, learning, and changing that you experience growth. When you think about significant questions such as, "In what way is your walk with God closer this year than last?" or, "How are you a better leader today than six months ago?" you position yourself to self-assess your growth—or lack thereof.

  Leadership growth is enhanced by your receptivity to coaching, correction, and change. Wise coaches are great gifts because they can both encourage you and point out areas that need improvement.

- It keeps your heart tender.

  When the Holy Spirit prompts you with a reproof, you have a choice in that moment to follow or dismiss. Or if it's a bigger issue, to obey or disobey. Following keeps your heart tender, while dismissing tends to harden your heart.

  The same is true in the human realm. A good picture of this is when there is a problem in your marriage. If your spouse talks to you about something you do that is hurtful but you blow it off, your heart tends to become hardened toward your spouse's feelings. In contrast, to be receptive and respond accordingly in love keeps your heart tender, and the result is usually a better relationship.

- It allows you to hear from God.

  A hardened heart that rejects correction is not only less responsive to God, but over time, it makes it harder to hear his voice. I'm not suggesting that God would stop talking to you, but to a degree, you may have tuned him out. Perhaps you didn't do it intentionally, but the result is that your ability to receive God's wisdom is jeopardized.

  > "Do not be wise in your own eyes; fear the LORD and shun evil." (Proverbs 3:7)

  > "My son, do not despise the LORD's discipline, and do not resent his rebuke, because the LORD disciplines those he loves, as a father the son he delights in." (Proverbs 3:11–12)

- It increases your credibility and influence as a leader.

  The acceptance of a rebuke with a mature attitude is a mark of humility, and it increases the level of trust people place in you and your leadership. This certainly doesn't mean that you should become a doormat for anyone who is critical of you. However, it does imply that credibility comes from character, and character is derived in part from humility. It's about the willingness to admit you were wrong or made a mistake, and you are willing to change when needed. People will follow a leader like that!

Reflection: What was the last correction you received, and how did you respond?

Notes:

ENGAGE YOUR PURPOSE

> For it is by grace you have been saved, through faith—and this is not from yourselves, it is the gift of God—not by works, so that no one can boast. For we are God's handiwork, created in Christ Jesus to do good works, which God prepared in advance for us to do.
>
> —Ephesians 2:8–10

Patti and I have two adult children, and they couldn't be more different. One is a PC, and the other is a Mac. Seriously! Our daughter, Mackenzie, leans heavily into the arts through filmmaking. Our son, John-Peter, is a science guy who makes his living as a software engineer. God wired and gifted them differently because he had a different purpose in mind for each of them.

In the devotion titled, "Accept Your Divine Assignment," the focus is the purpose of all Christians. In this devotion, the focus is your unique purpose.

The goal is not to create a narrow or rigid lane to accomplish God's purpose for you. Rather, it's to free you up to embrace a uniquely designed purpose where you can live and lead as the best version of yourself. The big idea here is to think and dream with God.

My friend Bob was uniquely created to design and build some of the most incredible guitars on this planet. He's passionate about his work and incredibly good at it. Anyone who knows him couldn't imagine Bob doing anything else. From the days when he was a starving luthier to now, decades later, by any measure Bob is very successful. But success wasn't his driving goal. His goal was always to build the best guitars. It's just in him.

What's in you? What did God's handiwork place inside you to make a mark in this world and for eternity? This doesn't mean you get to start out at your ideal. It may take years or even decades, just as it did for Bob. But here's the key question: Are you headed in the right direction?

Do you know how God has designed you, wired you, and gifted you? Do you have a clear sense of his vision for you and your life's work? If you don't or aren't sure, don't panic, but begin to focus on this subject. And if you do have a sense of your unique purpose, have your friends, family, peers, and mentors affirmed that purpose?

I have known my purpose for decades. It's encompassed in only three words: "Build the Church." That may sound more universal than unique, and if that were the end, I would agree, but the method is equally clear. My purpose is to build the Church through four avenues: leading, coaching, writing, and teaching. And it becomes especially unique when I add my priority system to it. I know my work has little to do with the creative arts, finance, technology, and so on, all of which, however, are critical to the success of any church. My priority system leans into leadership development, staffing, teamwork, culture, and strategy.

Can you see how that is very specific yet has lots of room to breathe? Now let me say this again: It took decades to get to the place where that's all I do, but the journey of growth and discovery has been wonderful.

Perhaps the path to your purpose has been fuzzy or evolved over time. That's okay! Sometimes trying new things illuminates new skills and passions we never would have recognized or embraced without trying a new path God placed in front of us. Grab hold of what God has for you, and make progress toward whatever is the right purpose for you.

Depending on your age and stage, some or all of the following guidelines will help you get where you want to go:

- Invest time in elevating your own self-awareness.
- Experiment with different ministry areas and ideas.
- Determine what tugs at your heart and what burdens you have for others.
- Don't worry about working outside your "zone" if you are learning and growing.
- Don't rush the process.
- Make sure you have at least one or two coaches/mentors who are honest with you.
- Talk with God regularly, asking him to make himself clear to you.

Reflection: Can you confidently answer the question of your purpose? If yes, are you where you want to be? If no, what is your next step?

Notes:

MERGE POWER, LOVE, AND LEADERSHIP

> For this reason I kneel before the Father, from whom every family in heaven and on earth derives its name. I pray that out of his glorious riches he may strengthen you with power through his Spirit in your inner being, so that Christ may dwell in your hearts through faith. And I pray that you, being rooted and established in love, may have power, together with all the LORD's holy people, to grasp how wide and long and high and deep is the love of Christ, and to know this love that surpasses knowledge—that you may be filled to the measure of all the fullness of God. Now to him who is able to do immeasurably more than all we ask or imagine, according to his power that is at work within us, to him be glory in the church and in Christ Jesus throughout all generations, for ever and ever! Amen.
>
> —Ephesians 3:14–21

The apostle Paul packed so much into this prayer. It's like a Christian manifesto for spiritual leaders.

Paul's humility and reverence for God are quickly evident. I imagine he is on his knees praying, acknowledging the grace of God, and asking on the behalf of others that they may be strengthened with power through the Spirit of God. The purpose? That they and you and I may know Christ is with us, residing in our hearts.

Paul then breaks the prayer down into bite-sized pieces.

- "Being rooted and established in love"
- "You may have power"
- In order to grasp the majesty and fullness of Jesus's love.

And finally, Paul gives the incredible benediction: To the one who amazes us and is able to do wildly beyond anything we can dream of, in alignment with his power that is in us, to him be the glory!

Spiritual leadership always starts with love. After love, power can be added. Jesus's sacrifice makes it possible for your ministry to come alive. He adds the power, and power guided by love is transformative. Power without love is tyrannical.

Perhaps you knew a bully in the neighborhood or a teacher who was unreasonable and unfair or a "church boss" who was oppressive. Pictures of power without love are plentiful. In contrast, the kindness and strength of a leader who demonstrates the love of Christ is truly life-giving. Without this, power tends to corrupt. Then even the most moral of leaders can fall prey to greed, fame, personal gain, immorality, or the love of money.

As a leader, you have authority by position, and you have spiritual power by relationship. It is the closeness of the relationship you maintain with Jesus that enables the power of the Holy Spirit within you to do good.

A pastor I know and respect is compelled by compassion to make a difference in the issue of hunger among school-aged children in his community. A heartbreaking number of kids there have only one meal a day when school is not in session. He is using his influence along with the love and resources of his congregation to make a difference. The good news is that we can tell stories like this one. What story are you part of, or what story do you want to be part of next?

Ask yourself what people groups or causes tug at your heart. What projects have you participated in that made a difference for Jesus? Your answer is most likely connected to the next chapter of your story, either personally or corporately. Spend some time asking God if it's his will and timing to clear a path or open a door for you.

The beauty of this passage does not begin with the good you can do with your influence. Rather, it begins with knowing the overwhelming love of God. Delight in that. Drink it in. Depend on it. In fact, not only is it about the love of God, it's about what *he* can do, not you. It's his power in and through you.

- Jesus's love nurtures your soul.
  Take a moment to reflect on the extraordinary love that God has just for you. Thank God for the peace, joy, and inner strength you carry because of his love.

- Jesus's love guides your steps.
  When your life is guided by the values of love, sacrifice, and giving, you have established a context and direction for your ministry.

Reflection: How has the love of Christ shaped the use of your influence these past three months?

Notes:

EMBRACE THE GIFT OF WISDOM

> If any of you lacks wisdom, you should ask God, who gives generously to all without finding fault, and it will be given to you. But when you ask, you must believe and not doubt, because the one who doubts is like a wave of the sea, blown and tossed by the wind.
>
> —James 1:5–6

Leadership will often present you with dilemmas such as:

"Letting this staff member go seems like the right decision, but it will be a very unpopular one."

"The new building project has lost momentum and giving is under budget. This situation is so complex that I really don't know what to do."

"We're in a meeting tomorrow about whether or not we should close a campus. It seems like a no-win scenario, but the right thing to do."

Can you relate to any of these dilemmas? Each requires wisdom to know how to handle the decision that needs to be made. In fact, wisdom is the great ally of any leader, and we need it on a daily basis. The need for wisdom isn't just for the big decisions; it's also for everyday life. Yet so often wisdom can seem to elude us. So how do we get a hold of it? It is a matter of asking God for it.

One of my favorite stories in the Bible is of Solomon asking God for wisdom:

> "Now, LORD my God, you have made your servant king in place of my father David. But I am only a little child and do not know how to carry out my duties. Your servant is here among the people you have chosen, a great people, too numerous to count or number. So give your servant a discerning heart to govern your people and to distinguish between right and wrong. For who is able to govern this great people of yours?" The Lord was pleased that Solomon had asked for this. So God said to him, "Since you have asked for this and not for long life or wealth for yourself, nor have asked for the death of your enemies but for discernment in administering justice, I will do what you have asked. I will give you a wise and discerning heart, so that there will never have been anyone like you, nor will there ever be." (1 Kings 3:7–12)

James 1:5 from our key passage today also confirms that we must ask for wisdom, but when God gives it to us, actually leading out of his wisdom can be complex. For example, we might face resistance from others, have limited resources to accomplish it, feel some fear or a lack of confidence about moving forward, or be unsure about the timing of the situation. These are normal hesitations, but we do well to remember that God is both the giver of wisdom and the rewarder of those who walk in it.

Scripture suggests at least two ways to deal with any complexities you might have to confront:

- Demonstrate your love for God.
  Back in our story about Solomon, we read he, "showed his love for the LORD by walking according to the instructions given him by his father David" (1 Kings 3:3). Your love for God is not about performance, perfection, or how big your church is. It's about your daily relationship of faith, grace, and obedience expressed in love to others. That's a truth you can rest in.

- Overcome doubt.
  James 1:6 says that we must believe and not doubt. Trusting God isn't always easy, and doubt causes us to question the wisdom we have been given. You can be encouraged to remember that wisdom is one of the things God promises to give if you ask.

I'm so grateful that both in the James passage and the story about Solomon, God's grace is clear. James says, "you should ask God, who gives generously to all without finding fault" (James 1:5). And 1 Kings 3:3 notes, "except that he [Solomon] offered sacrifices and burned incense on the high places." Clearly that was not pleasing to God, but God saw the bigger picture of Solomon's heart. God does not base today's wisdom on yesterday's mistakes and failures. That is such a gift to all of us who lead. Don't exclude yourself from this gift. Perhaps God gave you wisdom in a certain situation, but you dismissed it. Perhaps at another time, he again gave you wisdom, but you didn't use it well. Today you can ask for new and fresh wisdom. Today you can continue to demonstrate your love for God by not doubting his promises.

Reflection: What do you need God's wisdom for today? Ask him.

Notes:

FIND GOD IN THE WAITING

> I remain confident of this: I will see the goodness of the LORD in the land of the living. Wait for the LORD; be strong and take heart and wait for the LORD.
>
> —Psalm 27:13–14

Patience is perhaps one of the most unpopular among the godly traits we aspire to attain. Yesterday I walked into a bank to have money wired and was told the wait would be an hour, and it would be best to come back. I wondered for a moment if we had reverted to the dark ages. It took me a moment, but I did realize that the bank manager was being honest and courteous so that I did not waste my time.

We live in a lightning-fast world. If we have to wait more than five seconds for a website to load or an app to fully open, frustration kicks in. When you text someone and he or she doesn't respond in minutes, you might be tempted to wonder why. Businesses even cater to our culture of immediacy when we can have nearly anything shipped to our doorstep in a day or two.

Yet things in life that really matter take time. When it comes to the development of a baby, nine months is nine months. Developing a leader is not a microwave endeavor either. It's more like a Crock-Pot. And waiting on the Lord for answers and solutions may seem like forever, but scripture calls us to wait. These things simply take time.

The essence of waiting is twofold. First, to wait is to acknowledge that we can't do what is truly meaningful without God. And second, we can't rush eternity. Life change has a timeline that must be played out. The psalmist opens by declaring his confidence in the goodness of God, and the instruction is clear: Be strong and wait.

God did not leave us without help. It is not surprising that patience is one of the fruits of the Spirit listed in Galatians 5:22. The Holy Spirit gives us the ability to wait.

Psalm 37 teaches us not to worry when facing difficult situations, instead, to be still and wait patiently for God. "Be still before the LORD and wait patiently for him; do not fret when people succeed in their ways, when they carry out their wicked schemes" (Psalm 37:7).

Candidly, that scripture isn't always easy for me to accept. I know it's right, but I want to do *something*. There is a tension here. We are instructed to wait patiently and not fret, but how do we know what to do while we wait or when our emotions try to interfere?

It's important to know that waiting is not the same as surrendering or being passive. Waiting is about not getting out in front of God, not about sitting in surrender. Think about the power of prayer alone. That is far from surrender or doing nothing!

Have you ever hoped, prayed, and wanted your church to grow faster? If yes, you would be among the 99.9 percent who say, "Of course." Yet God can't be rushed. Then the tension kicks in: "What if the waiting is about my level of leadership or spiritual maturity?"

The big question is, "Am I waiting on God, or is he waiting on me?" Patience in these situations is a two-way street and can be complex to discern. There have been times when God couldn't give me more because I couldn't handle it. He demonstrated his patience and forbearance with me. There have also been times when I really was ready but God wasn't. He knows better than I do.

How to keep moving while remaining patient:

- Keep growing in spiritual maturity.

  The need for your continued spiritual maturity may be greater than it appears. Like a medical doctor who doesn't take care of his or her health or a car mechanic who neglects his own vehicle, it's surprising how many church leaders don't focus on their own growth because their time is invested in others. A prime example is if most of your Bible reading and study is to prepare for others rather than to prepare yourself.

- Keep growing in your leadership.

  There have been times when I've asked God for a great outpouring of spiritual harvest, and nothing seems to happen. Looking back, if God had answered that prayer, I would not have been able to handle it.

My passion is developing spiritual leaders, so as a leadership coach, I know that no matter how great a leader anyone is, there is room for growth. What area of your leadership needs to be strengthened over the next few months?

- Don't get ahead of God.

  Most leaders run fast and run hard. How about you? Does your drive occasionally cause you to get in front of your own headlights? Wait for God. The truth is, he is actually ahead of you and has your best interests in mind. God wants to bless your church, and he's working on things you are not yet aware of.

Wait. Be patient. I don't like it when someone says that to me either. I want to be patient while waiting to launch the next campus or hire a new team member, but at times it's difficult when I want to see progress and growth now. However, I know I need to wait on God, keep growing, and do the next right thing. Can you relate?

Reflection: What are you wrestling with that requires more patience? Are you waiting on God, or is he waiting on you?

Notes:

BUILD PURPOSEFUL UNITY

> So Christ himself gave the apostles, the prophets, the evangelists, the pastors and teachers, to equip his people for works of service, so that the body of Christ may be built up until we all reach unity in the faith and in the knowledge of the Son of God and become mature, attaining to the whole measure of the fullness of Christ.
>
> —Ephesians 4:11–13

Why is it that an independent spirit comes so easily, but unity in spirit and action among the body of Christ is so challenging? The answer is because both positive and negative responses exist. For example, on the negative side, the answer could be pride or ego that results in doing what you want to do regardless of the impact on others. On the positive side, it could be having the courage to take a risk to speak up for the sake of unity when others won't.

The issue becomes clear when divisiveness reveals its ugly presence, and the resulting lack of unity hurts the church. Division in the body of believers is a chief tool of the enemy. As a leader, it's your responsibility to fight for unity by leading the way.

A board member of a church with about five hundred in weekend attendance was angry with the pastor for releasing his son-in-law from the pastoral staff. He intentionally stirred up trouble, and dissention grew quickly among the board members. Some of the members of the church were also upset, but their reactions seemed to be reasonable. After all, they didn't know all the facts and were just sticking up for their friend.

This board member and one other member of the board of eleven voted against the pastor's decision. The pastor asked them to align with the others as a team. In the moment, they agreed but later changed their minds.

Emotions began to rise as the tension in the church increased. The board member attacked the pastor personally by challenging his integrity. The pastor was so hurt and angry that he followed in kind by releasing the board member from the board. It all happened in less than two weeks. It was a mess to say the least.

Stories like this one are all too common. The important questions are why did it happen and how could it have been prevented? On a personal level, how do you think you would have responded?

We all respond differently when hurt. Some power up and attack back. Others shut down and pull back. Others seek allies to help them defend their views.

When someone hurts you or attacks your leadership agenda, what might you need to change in order to make unity the focus of your response?

- Before you think strategically, think personally.
  This is a time for you and God to connect on something really important.

- Check your heart first.
  When God wants you to align with him, what is your first and most common response? And now the tough questions: How do you handle it when you disagree with God? Or perhaps you agree but don't like what he is saying to you?

Whatever is in your heart leaks into the culture of the church you lead. That doesn't mean you are responsible for the behaviors of every divisive person in your church. You couldn't possibly manage all the attitudes and squabbles. However, it does mean you're responsible for any differences between the overall spiritual temperature of the culture of your church and what you want to create. As a leader, your job is to help make things better, and I believe this starts by looking for ways to foster unity with the people around you.

Ephesians 4:3 makes it clear that maturity is the goal: "Make every effort to keep the unity of the Spirit through the bond of peace." This kind of maturity allows you to set your rights, privileges, and position aside to focus on what is best for others—even when you are hurt or angry. Unity is an incredible force for good, but it requires maturity to achieve it on a consistent basis.

Reflection: How would you describe the level of unity in your ministry? How has your leadership helped to shape it?

Notes:

PICK UP THE MINISTRY OF RECONCILIATION

> Therefore, if anyone is in Christ, the new creation has come: The old has gone, the new is here! All this is from God, who reconciled us to himself through Christ and gave us the ministry of reconciliation: that God was reconciling the world to himself in Christ, not counting people's sins against them. And he has committed to us the message of reconciliation. We are therefore Christ's ambassadors, as though God were making his appeal through us. We implore you on Christ's behalf: Be reconciled to God. God made him who had no sin to be sin for us, so that in him we might become the righteousness of God.
>
> —2 Corinthians 5:17–21

With forty years in leadership and forty-eight years as a follower of Jesus, it's hard to imagine or even remember being separated from God, but I was. We all were.

It was 1973 when I surrendered my heart to belief in Jesus as Savior. I was in my late teens, and it was an Easter Sunday service. I attended that morning probably more because of my interest in a girl than God. She was clear that she wouldn't date me unless I went to church, so I went. But the Holy Spirit was at work. The service was outdoors at a high school football stadium, and we all sat in the bleachers with the stage set up just across the track on the infield.

The service was great, but it wasn't the worship or the sermon or even the friendly people that captured me. It was the words painted on the traditional background of blue sky and lilies behind the choir. Three words completely grabbed my soul, "He is Risen!" The Holy Spirit simply whispered to me, *It's true*. That was it. Two words. But I didn't go forward at the invitation. It wasn't until the next day that I told my friend what happened. I asked her if I had to wait till next Easter to be saved. She smiled, kindly said no, and we prayed right then. I've never been the same since.

Being reconciled to God through Christ ended my eternal separation from God and launched my new life in Christ. Your story is different, but the outcome is the same. Not only did you experience reconciliation with God through Christ's sacrifice, you were also given a ministry of reconciliation. Together we are ambassadors of the message of reconciliation. What a privilege! Have you given much thought to the importance of your story lately?

- Your story keeps your heart hot toward God.
  Take a minute to reflect on your story. How did it happen for you? Can you remember your life before Christ? Can you imagine what your life would be like today without God?

  My life as a Christ follower and a Christian leader has been far from perfect, but at the same time, it's been infinitely better because of the work of Christ in me. My heart is humbled and grateful for God's grace, kindness, and favor. How about you?

- Your story keeps your heart hot toward others who are far from God.
  Your story of reconciliation helps your heart stay tender toward those who remain separated and distant from God. Your personal experience reminds you of the incredible gift you have received, and that gratitude compels you to tell others. But it's not always that easy, is it? Sometimes our hearts can change, especially under the pressure of leadership.

The heart is typically at the root of any problems we face when it comes to fulfilling our ministries of reconciliation. This is because the heart can be deceitful (Jeremiah 17:9), so be careful about these three possible heart issues:

- Complacency
  Over time, it's easier than you might think to get comfortable in the routine of ministry and drift from passion.

- Cynicism
  A complacent heart becomes cynical when church becomes routine and lackluster, and when you observe church happening under your leadership, and you no longer experience the joy you once had. This makes you begin asking questions like, "Does this really matter?" Then doubts arise.

- Hardness
  If cynicism is allowed to live long enough, your heart becomes hard. That doesn't necessarily mean you've overtly sinned, but it means you're no longer responding to the gentle prompts of God.

Do everything possible to keep your heart tender, responsive, and hot for God.

Reflection: What are you doing to cultivate your heart's passion toward the reconciliation of others to God?

Notes:

CONFESS FOR THE GOOD OF YOUR SOUL

> Blessed is the one whose transgressions are forgiven, whose sins are covered. Blessed is the one whose sin the LORD does not count against them and in whose spirit is no deceit. When I kept silent, my bones wasted away through my groaning all day long. For day and night your hand was heavy on me; my strength was sapped as in the heat of summer. Then I acknowledged my sin to you and did not cover up my iniquity. I said, "I will confess my transgressions to the LORD." And you forgave the guilt of my sin.
>
> —Psalm 32:1–5

Sin makes us want to hide, pretend, and cover things up, but confession provides the avenue by which we experience freedom and grace. Once when I was a teenager, a buddy and I were driving too fast for a winding road along the side of a cliff and lost control of my mom's car. Going into a sharp turn, the car spun in a circle and slammed into a metal mile-marker right at the very edge of the cliff. Had we gone over, it would probably have been the end for both of us. Driving like that was stupid but not a sin. Lying to my mom about it when we got home was the sin. I carried that burden for a very long time and finally, as an adult, confessed to her what happened to her Ford Maverick those many years ago. She looked at me and said, "Thank you for telling me, but I knew the instant you told me."

In Psalm 32, it is obvious that David felt the burden of his silence, his secret, and his lack of confession. The presence of God was heavy upon him. I imagine he must have experienced that as simultaneously good and bad. On the one hand, it was good to know that God was with him, and yet God's presence and the sense of conviction he felt was clearly overwhelming.

The value of confession:

- Confession finds its power in the cross and its reward in both freedom and joy. Confession brings the truth to light, and the truth leads us to love, grace, and forgiveness.
- Confession is connected to spiritual power because of the death and resurrection of Jesus. His blood cleanses us of sin and sets us free to live a life without pretense.
- Without confession, we carry unnecessary burdens and run the risk of our hearts slowly becoming hardened. The result of a hardened heart is lowered receptivity to the nudges, prompts, and voice of the Holy Spirit.

It's curious that as leaders we can teach this truth much easier than we can live it out. I believe this is because confession requires vulnerability and being known, which necessitates personal security within a leader. The payoff is that this level of authenticity allows us to better connect with others and be real with God.

We don't confess our shortcomings to God so he will know them; he already knows. We confess to own and acknowledge our wrongdoings, impure thoughts, or acts of disobedience. We confess to conquer pride and break bondage. Confession best begins with sorrow or remorse so that we are sincere and genuinely do not want to repeat the offense.

Many find that it's easier to confess to a holy and perfect God than to a fellow sinner. The good news is that confessing to God is the right thing. But scripture also calls for confession to one another (James 5:16). There is no specific formula that must be used.

Confession isn't always public; nor is it limited to one person at a time. Follow the Spirit's prompts.

Just like the coverup with my mom, confession to another human being you respect is difficult. You can feel embarrassed, judged, or rejected. But the truth is you will find acceptance and grace far more often than not. And the unburdening of your soul brings a freedom that produces great joy. Richard Foster said, "Confession begins in sorrow, but it ends in joy. There is celebration in the forgiveness of sins because it results in a genuinely changed life."[6]

In hindsight, I could have received my mom's grace immediately and not carried that burden—though as a consequence, I may have been grounded for a month. Even when we know that it doesn't work, it often seems easier to try to hide stuff. If we carry transgressions long enough, our souls can become dry and lack receptivity to the nudges of the Holy Spirit. Over time, that can erode our favor as a leader because it hardens our hearts. And when our hearts are hardened, it hinders us from hearing God. That's not a threat; that's an invitation. We have the opportunity to make anything right.

It is wise to protect the sensitivity of your soul, even to the little things. Sometimes a simple, "I'm sorry," in the moment to your friend, spouse, or even a stranger is a confession that allows you to continue to walk in freedom and joy.

Reflection: What burden are you carrying that you need to confess? What holds you back from confessing it today?

Notes:

---

[6] Richard J. Foster, *Celebration of Discipline: The Path to Spiritual Growth* (San Francisco: Harper Collins, 1978), 153.

VALUE ONE MORE LEADER

> Then he said to his disciples, "The harvest is plentiful but the workers are few."
>
> —Matthew 9:37

O ne of the great burdens of a leader is the shortage of "workers" who are committed to the purpose of the church. One of my most fervent prayers is for more leaders who are sold out to reaching people for Jesus. 12Stone Church, where I serve, is located in a suburb of Atlanta, Georgia, where there are hundreds of churches and hundreds of thousands of people who do not have a relationship with Jesus.

The sobering truth is that if every church in Atlanta were filled multiple times over, there would still be countless thousands who do not follow Jesus. Regardless of the actual numbers, I'm sure this is also true to some extent for your church as well.

If you are in local church leadership or ministry of any kind, there is no doubt you share this burden. In fact, you likely carry it at two levels. The first is at a heart level, feeling broken for the lost; and the second is at a practical level, feeling the pressure that comes with needing more leaders to reach the lost.

The thought of needing more leaders can become anything from overwhelming to paralyzing. Where do you start? How do you keep up? And what happens when your leaders quit? The principle of "one more" is highly encouraging. Adding just one more leader can change your church, no matter the size.

Think of it this way, the senior pastor is one leader, and the difference your pastor makes is enormous. You are one leader; consider the difference you make. Each volunteer who rises to leadership makes a big difference. Every time you add just one more leader, it's a game-changer.

A senior pastor I know at a church of about four hundred in attendance was feeling the burden that's all too common. After losing several key volunteer leaders because a local company went out of business, and losing one staff member at the same time, he was really feeling the pressure for help. He felt overwhelmed because he was focused on the need for many instead of the potential for one, one at a time, and the difference each one would make.

The pastor began to pray, and two things happened. A new couple moved into his community and visited the church. They were mature Christian leaders who jumped right into student ministry. And the pastor reached out to an up-and-coming young leader he had mentored but hadn't interacted with in a while. The young leader needed more development but could begin immediately as an apprentice. The need for help wasn't completely resolved, but these three people felt like thirty to the pastor.

God answers this prayer for leaders in so many ways:

- You can pray for a first-time visitor to be a leader who is ready to lead. God does that.
- You can challenge a person who is serving but not leading to step up to the next level.
- You can select someone with potential and help develop others to become potential leaders on your team.

Developing leaders is a cumulative process, and it's slow, like a Crock-Pot, not fast like a microwave. But if you stay with it, the compounding effects are staggering. Over time, the formula begins to change from one at a time to two at a time to four at a time, and the results not only lift your spirits but advance the mission.

The spiritual secret to one more leader is your passion for the harvest. That's what keeps you going. The idea of having a bigger church won't motivate you for the long haul because bigger isn't better unless it's healthy and growing according to the right metrics. And no amount of focus on leadership development, as important as it is, will keep you going without it being deeply connected to a larger mission—your vision for the lost.

The verse just before today's scripture captures this idea. Matthew 9:36 says, "When he saw the crowds, he had compassion on them, because they were harassed and helpless, like sheep without a shepherd."

Your compassion for people is a powerful spiritual secret that provides great energy to help you find and equip one more leader at a time.

Reflection: What effort at a heart level and in the spiritual realm can you invest toward your next leader?

Notes:

CULTIVATE THE COURAGE TO CONFRONT

> Instead, speaking the truth in love, we will grow to become in every respect the mature body of him who is the head, that is, Christ.
> —Ephesians 4:15

Our staff often jokes with each other about who is a "grace person" or a "truth person." We all have a bent and bias toward one side over the other. Those who lean toward truth draw clear lines between right and wrong, and they don't hesitate to let others know their interpretations of situations or issues. In contrast, those who lean toward grace are generally more comfortable with moving the lines and accepting tones of gray depending on the circumstances. This doesn't represent strength or weakness or mean one is better than the other. Both are clearly represented in scripture, and both sides require courage.

In which direction do you lean? Your answer is important because it determines much of how you approach tough conversations when you need to confront someone about a difficult issue. No leader enjoys dealing with conflict. However, there is always good that comes from the need for confrontation:

- Difficult conversations with others are usually opportunities for your personal growth as a leader.
- Confrontation almost always goes better than you anticipate.
- Your courage to confront for the good of others elevates your influence as a leader.

Years ago I was leading a small group of men, and we discussed the topic of financial generosity. The conversation quickly moved to questions about tithing in general and then more pointedly to questions about leadership and giving, such as, "Is the expectation for generosity different for a Christian who is not in a position of leadership?" And, "Are the standards for a leader who is responsible for setting the example higher than for others?" Needless to say, it was an intense discussion, and the grace guys and truth guys polarized in minutes.

One of the guys in the group indicated that he tithed and believed it was not an option, especially for a leader. However, his brother had recently sought my advice about how to best help with some financial stresses he witnessed in his life without embarrassing him, and during the course of that conversation, he mentioned that his brother doesn't support the idea of tithing. Perhaps if I were more of a "truth person," I'd have confronted him right then and there with the group, but I thought I should probably do it privately to extend more grace. I was not looking forward to it. I was a young pastor and unsure what I thought about the appropriateness of confronting a leader about giving. Two things, however, pushed me forward. One, I cared about him. And two, the group had established an "iron sharpens iron" permission for accountability with each other.

A couple of weeks later, we met for lunch. After some small talk, I brought up the discussion about generosity and tithing, which he remembered. I said, "Hey, I want you to know I'm aware of your real thoughts regarding tithing because your brother asked me how he could be helpful to you financially, and the matter came up." We then had a difficult conversation about truth-telling mixed with the pressures of financial stress on a marriage.

I did not want to press him further about trusting God with his finances because I felt compassion for his situation. And he was already embarrassed about not being honest in the group. However, I sensed the Holy Spirit prompting me: *Don't waste this opportunity. It's not about money; it's about trust and his love for me.*

His response, which is not uncommon among people struggling to trust God in this area, was to become defensive as he argued that tithing was an Old Testament idea. I responded by saying the New Testament teachings call for even greater generosity. I knew a debate would distract us from the real issue, so I gently asked, "Friend, what do you think God wants you to do?" He stopped, got quiet, and his heart softened as we spoke about it together.

Conversations like this one require courage—primarily because we don't know how they will go. That lunch might have made him angry, damaged our friendship, or even caused him to leave the church. Yet we must engage in these conversations with one another on a regular basis because accountability is one way God keeps us aligned with truth and walking in righteousness.

It was the combination of truth and grace that gave me courage. God's Word makes the truth clear, and God's grace within me allowed my love for him to come through clearly.

Reflection: What elements of grace and truth is God calling you to remember regarding a tough conversation he has asked you to have?

Notes:

KEEP A DILIGENT WATCH

> Be shepherds of God's flock that is under your care, watching over them—not because you must, but because you are willing, as God wants you to be; not pursuing dishonest gain, but eager to serve; not lording it over those entrusted to you, but being examples to the flock.
>
> —1 Peter 5:2–3

Patti and I have been blessed with our first grandchild, a little girl named Anza. She's fifteen months old at the time I'm writing this devotion. My daughter, Mackenzie, and son-in-law, Jacob, are such good parents, protective and loving of their little one. We all nurture and watch over Anza with great care.

When we were in Destin, Florida, recently, we invited the "kids" down to join us for a couple of days. It was Anza's first time in a swimming pool and the ocean, so we watched over her with a careful eye.

Parenting—and grandparenting—is a great picture of the heart of a shepherd. Some of the functions are different, but the heart is what makes the difference. First Peter 5:2 says, "not because you must, but because you are willing." In other words, shepherd others because you *want* to. It's not always easy, and some days are very difficult. Yet, it's so worth the investment.

There are three more instructions in this passage:

- Pursue what is best for those you shepherd.

  Your intent is always what's best for those you serve, but over the years, I've seen what fatigue, pressure, and setbacks can do to even the best of leaders. We don't shepherd for what we can get out of it. However, for example, if you are in great need of volunteers, it's easy to innocently experience a shift in motivation.

  Motivation is not the same as motive. Your motives reflect the intent of your heart, while your motivation reflects the things that move you. Yes, it's a thin line between the two, but there is a difference. That's why we can feel true in our motives but slip in our motivations when under pressure. Motives tend to reflect the big picture of our hearts, and motivations tend to reflect what's in play in the moment. Pay attention to both.

- Use your authority with grace and humility.

  The Message translates 1 Peter 5:3 this way: "Not bossily telling others what to do, but tenderly showing them the way."

  I was coaching a pastor in a large church because he struggled with how he came across to his team. He was a good leader and cared about people, but the staff and volunteers felt he overused his authority. In other words, they respected him because they had to, but they didn't like him. They believed he knew what he was doing but did not sense that he cared for them. The message he kept receiving was, "We don't feel shepherded."

  After some discussion, the adjustment was relatively easy. He began inviting staff and groups of volunteers to his house to grill, and he was the grill master. This gave them the opportunity to see a different side of him, and they all had a blast while experiencing his genuine hospitality!

He still leads with an appropriate amount of authority, but grace and humility come through much more clearly. It made all the difference in the world.

- Lead by your own good example.
  The best parents lead by example. Good leaders do the same. We have a residency program at 12Stone Church. It's a two-year, postcollege ministry leadership training program. The residents have classroom training every week and about twenty hours of on-the-job training where they practice leadership and ministry. In all this, they learn and absorb the most by watching their leaders lead.

  You are always being watched. Don't feel threatened by that; use it for the good of those you lead. You don't have to be perfect, but do your best to lead the way. For example, if you want your team to be on time for a meeting, you must be on time. It's that simple.

Reflection: In what ways do you currently see yourself serving well as a shepherd? Is there an area you have forgotten or needs to be improved?

Notes:

AFFIRM BIG LEADERSHIP PRAYERS

> Listen to my words, LORD, consider my lament. Hear my cry for help, my King and my God, for to you I pray. In the morning, LORD, you hear my voice; in the morning I lay my requests before you and wait expectantly.
> —Psalm 5:1–3

Imagine an invitation to talk with a king or president of a country anytime you desired. Not only were you invited to engage with that leader whenever you wanted, he would also listen to you and respond! That would be extraordinary. That's the invitation God gives you with even greater power, authority, and, more important, love for you.

As a Christian leader, you no doubt understand this invitation and spend time in prayer. But is your prayer life what you want it to be? Most leaders know prayer is a game changer because it strengthens our souls and leadership abilities. However, we also face many potential hurdles that can trip us up and prevent a powerful prayer life. Whether it's an emergency phone call, a project with which your kids need help, running late for a big meeting, travel, or a broken water heater, the distractions are endless. Life always has a way of interrupting what is truly important with things that are urgent.

On the other hand, sometimes you fail to engage in a consistent and fruitful prayer life because you've just slipped out of the habit. More than one pastor has confided that he missed praying for days because he was so discouraged about his ministry. Others just dash out the door because they have so much to do and love doing it. How about you?

I know the invitation and opportunity to pray can be overwhelming. The needs are so many—from visions and dreams to hopes and healings. We pray for salvation, the personal needs of those we shepherd, finances, the community, hunger and poverty, specific ministries, staff, our own families and personal needs, and, of course, there's no end to this list either. But don't waste the privilege of prayer. It's your most powerful resource as a leader.

If we're honest about the practicalities, we acknowledge that we can't pray for everything. So where do we start? The purpose of this devotion is not to limit your prayers. You can pray for anything anytime. But some prayers are positioned to give big-picture enhancement to your specific prayers and leadership. They bring life, energy, and strength to what you do as a leader.

Seven topics for big leadership prayers:

- Bold faith
  I've never considered my faith to be big and bold. My faith is unwavering and sure, but I think a more bold and growing faith is needed, not only to pray with strength and belief, but to lead in the same way.

- Kingdom courage
  The fears and insecurities that are common to leaders require courage to overcome. God provides courage as we pray and take action to demonstrate our faith.

  Kingdom courage is focused specifically on the needs of the kingdom centered on God's purpose in Matthew 28:18–20.

- Servant influence
  We are servants of God entrusted to serve others just as Jesus modeled for us. That's a big leadership prayer. When our hearts are inclined toward serving for the good of others, we can be trusted with more influence.

- Personal strength
  The larger your ministry grows, the greater the need for personal strength. This includes physical stamina, consistent character, and spiritual tenacity.

  As a leader, you need different things on different days. There are days when substantial physical energy is needed to press on, and there are other days when spiritual perseverance is needed to resist temptation. There are still other times when you face a spiritual battle, and great strength is required. Those who hope in the LORD will renew their strength (Isaiah 40:31).

- Pure wisdom
  James 3:17 says, "But the wisdom that comes from heaven is first of all pure; then peace-loving, considerate, submissive, full of mercy and good fruit, impartial and sincere." This verse gives us great insight into God's wisdom, and the word "pure" has always stood out to me. God's wisdom is connected to the things that are in perfect alignment with his will. This wisdom is unblemished, perfect, and not contaminated by the world. It gives us uncommon clarity that steers us strategically and directionally.

- Unmerited favor
  Grace is the unmerited favor of God and the basis of our salvation. It's the beautiful gift of eternal life we want and pray for others to have.

But grace doesn't stop at salvation. Even though as Christians we are new creations (2 Corinthians 5:17), sin is still a reality. Grace is the gift that covers our humanity as we lead. This is not an excuse to sin, but it is encouragement that when we do fail, God's grace is real.

- Spiritual authority
  I'm sure you would agree that the last thing you want to do is lead in your own power. We know how futile that is. Your prayer is for spiritual authority that allows the power of the Holy Spirit to be fully engaged in and through your leadership.

Please don't be overwhelmed by these prayers, wondering, *How can I add all these to my already lengthy list?* Here's a good approach. Pray one of these seven big prayers one day each week and see what God does.

"Devote yourselves to prayer, being watchful and thankful." (Colossians 4:2)

Reflection: How could you best leverage one of these big prayers for your leadership and your church?

Notes:

TWENTY LEADERSHIP PRAYERS FOR YOU

As a church leader you pray daily for others, and that's good. However, these prayers are for you. They are meant as prayers you can take directly to God.

There are times when a written prayer can unlock a blockage, enhance depth, or just help you get started when you don't have the words. You can pray these just as they are or use them as a springboard to personalize each sentence to fit your needs in the moment.

COURAGE

> Lord God, I need courage to lead in a way that advances the church, aligns with your will, and brings glory to your name. Help me sustain the courage to stand up for what is right, proclaim the full truth of your Word, and to fight for those who cannot fight for themselves. May a spirit of courage fill me, overcome my fears, and enable me to take risks and make tough decisions that move the church forward. When my courage wanes in the moment, remind me of your presence that I may continue to press on and lead well for the good of the church. Amen.

FAITH

Jesus, grant me great faith for the work you have called me to do so that what you have placed in my heart may come to pass. Strengthen me that I may inspire others to greater faith. During the times my faith falters, increase my faith. I know the lack of faith among your disciples frustrated you, so help me stay strong. I know you are with me, but the load can get heavy. I know you have called me, but it's not always easy to see your hand at work. Help me see bigger, believe greater, and lead larger. Amen.

WISDOM

Holy Spirit, grant me wisdom that I may discern the things I do not understand. Help me to gain your perspective and know what to do. Make your will clear for the decisions I need to make. Speak to me in the moment while I lead meetings, engage in challenging conversations, and stand up to teach. I pray you will be the divine editor of my thoughts and words. Teach me to pray in accordance with the Father's will, and grant me sensitivity to hear your voice. May my heart never be hardened or block your prompts. Instead, may I always cherish your wisdom and seek it daily. Amen.

DEEP REST

Father in heaven, I'm so grateful for the ministry you have given me. Yet I confess that I can become weary. There are times when even a good night's sleep and a day off do not reach deep into my soul for the renewing rest I need. When stresses and pressures cause me to reach my human limits, teach me to lean into you for a soul-level kind of rest, the kind that cannot be found by human means alone. Speak to my heart that I may sense your closeness. As I seek to be aware of your presence throughout the day, walk with me and give me rest. Amen.

CONFIDENCE

Jesus, place within me the confidence that you are truly with me in my daily leadership and to believe in myself according to the gifts and talents you have given me. May I not shrink back or second-guess what I know you have placed in my heart and mind to do. Thank you for the mentors who believe in me and my leadership; they are true gifts, but Father, it's you I depend on. May I never be overconfident and fall prey to pride or slide into a lack of confidence and dishonor how you have designed me. Instill within me an authentic and consistent confidence that reflects both a humble spirit and the spiritual gifts you gave me. Amen.

PEACE

God of peace, my heart finds its way to worry and anxiousness more than I would like. I trust you fully, but day-to-day life trips me up. I can worry about my kids, church finances, or who will or won't come back to church next Sunday. I know worry is pointless, but in the moment, it's very real. If you choose not to lift the load, would you please replace the worry with peace? Breathe your peace that is beyond human understanding into my soul that I may lead with poise, confidence, and a nonanxious presence. May your peace in me bring peace to others. Amen.

VISION

Jesus, you have taught me that vision begins with a burden. It seems like a dangerous prayer to ask you to place a burden in my soul with something so moving that I'm compelled and consumed to act, but that's my heart's desire. Please place deep within me your vision to lead your church forward along with a burden that demands action. May the vision be aligned with your will and pleasing to you. Help me communicate that vision with the hope of a better future. May the vision be large enough to need more leaders. Send us godly leaders and help us raise up spiritual leaders to reach more people! Amen.

HOPE

Heavenly Father, my hope is in you, and I praise you and thank you for my salvation. Thank you for the hope and promise of eternal life. Forgive me for any doubts on difficult days, and fill me with your full assurance. May my hope in eternity be so strong and so true that it is contagious to those I serve and lead. May my hope bring life and encouragement to those who feel hopeless. Jesus, there are so many today who have little joy or meaning in life short of the best they can manufacture in the moment. Life seems empty to many. Help me lead in such a way that they find life to the full in you! Amen.

RESILIENCE

Father, it seems like my ministry is filled with one problem after another. I'm not complaining because I know that solving problems is core to making progress. But there are so many setbacks. You've called and equipped me to be a problem solver, but I need the level of resilience that only you can give. Strengthen me, Lord, and make me a resilient leader that can bounce back from setbacks with renewed energy, vision, and enthusiasm. I need greater resilience to think bigger, lead stronger, and maintain a consistent positive spirit that will encourage others. Amen.

COMPASSION

Jesus, I'm so grateful for your compassion. Your care for me is so clear through both concern about my needs and lovingkindness in my daily life. Your father's heart reaches my heart and shows me the way to care for others. Jesus, increase my compassion for those in need, those who are marginalized, and for those who do not yet know your love. Grant me discernment to understand their real needs and to know who you want me to help. Help me to slow down in just the right moments in order to see and connect with each person to whom you want me to express genuine compassion. Amen.

PROTECTION

Father, protect me from those who set out to harm me, my family, my reputation, or the church I serve. It seems as though now more than ever, especially with the access social media affords, there are attacks that come my way, even from people who have never met me. At times I feel defenseless. I'm not a victim, and I trust you with my reputation. But I surely can't fight all my battles alone. Help me fight the right battles in the right way. May I be silent and turn the other cheek at the right times. Bring others to my side and intercessors on my behalf that I might serve you and my church well. Amen.

BOLDNESS

Father, I know you do not place within me a spirit of fear or timidity but one of power, love, and discipline. Help me never to back down and to always speak up for what is right according to the truth of your Word. Grant me the boldness to represent you and stand for biblical principles no matter what. May love always be the foundation of my boldness. May my boldness always be wrapped in kindness but propelled by unmistakable conviction. Father, I pray my boldness would lift your name. Amen.

LOVE

Father in heaven, love as an idea is easy to embrace. Love as an action is difficult to live up to on a consistent basis. It requires so much intentional effort and energy. Father, I pray that you enlarge my heart for people even more so that I may be renewed with the energy it takes to love even more. I want my love to be more than merely known, but felt, and result in changed lives. May the authenticity of my love start at home with my family, and may there be more than enough to overflow on others. Amen.

DISCIPLINE

Lord Jesus, I don't know exactly how to pray about this, but I ask that you help me increase my discipline or perhaps focus the discipline I do have. It seems like I should behave in a more disciplined manner rather than ask you to bless me with discipline. But I'm grateful I can ask you to help me do my part. I ask for discipline in my thinking, priorities, how I use my time and resources, and how I take care of my physical body so that I may have the needed energy to serve and lead others well. I pray that discipline does not become a legalistic taskmaster but a virtue that ultimately produces freedom and margin to live and lead better. Amen.

PURPOSE

God, you knew me before I was born, you know me in my innermost being, and you know when my days will be done. Thank you for creating me on purpose for a purpose. I pray that you would continue to make my path clear, direct my steps, and grant favor on my calling. Am I exactly where you want me to be and serving you to my fullest capacity? Fresh anointing, Lord, I pray! Thank you for the opportunities you give me to help more people know who you are. Thank you for inviting me to be part of building your Church. Amen.

HOLINESS

Jesus, the words, "be holy for I am holy," are both inspiring and at times overwhelming. How can I be like you? Yet that is the very thing you invite me to live up to! I know that it's only by your grace and through your blood that righteousness or holiness can be lived out. And yet my part of the process is to manage my will, my heart, and my obedience. My prayer is for purity in thought, motive, and behavior. I invite your Holy Spirit to fill me in a new and fresh way today. My heart and hands are open. Amen.

JOY

Lord, your joy is my strength! As a leader, I know the importance of my countenance and my ability to bring joy to others, but it has to begin in me. It must be genuine, and you are my source. Happiness from the world is short-lived while your joy is eternal. When joy eludes me, fill me again. On the difficult days may I remember your love and faithfulness. Even when I'm under attack or suffering, may I experience your joy. My desire is to carry that joy to others that they may be encouraged in the moment and drawn to you over time. Amen.

FAVOR

Heavenly Father, without your favor my ministry efforts are in vain. At best they are fleeting in nature. Eternal value and impact come only from your power. I ask for favor according to your will and to the benefit of the Church. I ask for favor to reach more people so they may know you! I need your favor in casting vision, developing leaders, having difficult conversations, and unleashing resources. I pray I never step outside the bounds of your cover, and that you are pleased with my stewardship of all that you have entrusted to me. Amen.

SPIRITUAL WARFARE

Jesus, protect me from the evil one. I know the battle isn't against flesh and blood but against the rulers, against the authorities, against the powers of this dark world, and against the spiritual forces of evil in the heavenly realms. Thank you for the spiritual armor you promised in Ephesians chapter 6. Help me to wear it as a true warrior. You have given me the power of prayer, the covering of Jesus's blood, and the Word, but sometimes the battle is still overpowering. Spiritual attack often comes my way before I teach, while on vacation when I need to rest, or in an important meeting. Give me strength, Jesus, to overcome the enemy's attacks. Amen.

FORGIVENESS

Jesus, you have clearly taught me to forgive, even seventy times seven times. You forgave me! Yet at times it can be so difficult to forgive others, especially those who are intentional about the problems they cause, the pain they bring, and the results that linger. Pretending there is no pain or consequence to deal with isn't honest or real, but I know there is a better way. Keep me tender by the amazing truth of how much you forgave in me and the price you paid for my freedom. I pray I am as grace-filled with others as you are with me. Amen.

SCRIPTURE INDEX

Scripture	Page	Scripture	Page
Psalm 5:1–3	132	John 14:16–17	57
Psalm 20:6–9	19	John 14:26–27	16
Psalm 27:13–14	110	John 15:5–8	4
Psalm 32:1–5	120	Acts 1:8	26
Psalm 34:4–8	38	Acts 4:31	44
Psalm 37:3–7	29	1 Corinthians 9:24–27	81
Psalm 89:1–8	61	2 Corinthians 5:17–21	117
Psalm 95:6–7	47	2 Corinthians 3:4–6	22
Psalm 100	8	2 Corinthians 12:9–10	1
Psalm 119:9–16	85	Galatians 6:9	65
Psalm 139:1-6	71	Ephesians 2:8–10	100
Psalm 141:5	96	Ephesians 3:14–21	103
Matthew 6:33–34	12	Ephesians 4:11–13	114
Matthew 7:12	93	Ephesians 4:15	126
Matthew 9:37	123	Ephesians 4:29	35
Matthew 11:28	68	Ephesians 6:10–18	41
Matthew 22:37–39	51	1 Timothy 3:1–10	75
Matthew 28:18–20	54	2 Timothy 3:16–17	78
Mark 10:42–45	32	James 1:5–6	106
Luke 9:23–24	89	1 Peter 5:2–3	129

OTHER RESOURCES BY DAN REILAND

BOOKS

Confident Leader! Become One, Stay One

> Every leader knows confidence is a vital part of leading well, but when challenges and setbacks overtake you, it's easy to lose your confidence. Thankfully, though, it can be strengthened. In *Confident Leader!* Dan presents a comprehensive and practical process to bring clarity to your identity, help you develop your character, and gain practical skills to increase your leadership confidence.

Amplified Leadership: 5 Practices to Establish Influence, Build People, and Impact Others for a Lifetime

> The key to reaching your ministry's maximum potential and accomplishing all that God has for you is developing strong leaders who will help advance your mission. In *Amplified Leadership*, Dan gives you a proven process that establishes spiritually mature leaders with practical skills. It includes valuable tips on how to establish relationships, engage followers, equip team members, coach apprentices, and mentor new leaders.

Shoulder to Shoulder: Strengthening Your Church by Supporting Your Pastor

Pastors have a tough job, and sometimes it can be a lonely one. Thankfully, most people want to support their pastors; however, they might just not know how to do it. Dan's book *Shoulder to Shoulder* helps laypeople understand the unique challenges their pastors may be facing and provides them with helpful ideas to make positive differences in their pastors' lives and contribute to the advancements of the visions for their churches.

*This book is particularly helpful for churches of five hundred people or less.

CURRICULUM

Joshua's Men Training Curriculum: A One-Year Process to Raise Up Spiritual Leaders

Joshua's Men is an intensive leadership training program for men in the local church. The curriculum's emphasis includes spiritual leadership, character development, and topics that increase influence for positive results at home, in the workplace, and at church. This curriculum is best implemented in the context of a small group setting, meeting monthly, and led by an experienced leader. It is available for download free of charge at resources.12Stone.church.

BLOG

The Pastor's Coach

> *The Pastor's Coach,* at danreiland.com, is a catalogue
> of Dan's leadership insights gleaned over four
> decades of ministry experience. His heart for
> pastors, along with his passion for developing and
> empowering leaders at every level, is evident in each
> post. Subscribe at danreiland.com.

Dan would love to hear from you. To share how you've been impacted
by *Leadership Alone Isn't Enough,* or to inquire about executive coaching
or church consulting, contact Dan at dan@danreiland.com.

ABOUT THE AUTHOR

Dan Reiland has been a pastor and leader for more than forty years. He served alongside John C. Maxwell for twenty years, first as executive pastor at Skyline Church and then as vice president of leadership and church development for INJOY Ministries. For the last twenty years, he has served as executive pastor with founding and senior pastor, Kevin Myers, of 12Stone® Church in Lawrenceville, Georgia.

Dan is the author of *Confident Leader! Amplified Leadership*, and *Shoulder to Shoulder*. He blogs regularly on *The Pastor's Coach* at danreiland.com. Dan is best known as a leader with a pastor's heart and a coach's instincts. He truly loves the local church and is described as one of the nation's most innovative church thinkers, a top church consultant, and an exceptional executive leadership coach. His passion is developing and empowering leaders who want to grow and are willing to take risks for the kingdom of God.

Dan and his wife, Patti, have two children, John-Peter and Mackenzie, who is married to Jacob, and a granddaughter, Anza. In his spare time, he enjoys time at the beach with Patti, grillin' and chillin' with his family, and playing the guitar.